The Edge of the Cliff

By

Marion G. Cochrane, M. B. E.

First Edition 2018

© Eli Press

ISBN-978-1-908-788-09-2

Printed by
Eli Press
121, Low Etherley, Bishop Auckland,
Co. Durham DL14 0HA

Contents

HOW I CAME TO WRITE THE STORY OF ROBERT COCHRANE

Dr. Robert Greenhill Cochrane (1899-1985) C.M.G., M.D.,F.R.C.S. D.T.M.&H. .

Most treasured award India, Kaiser-I-Hind. First class (Gold) in 1951 in India.

.

My Father-in-law, the subject of this book, was a giant in the field of leprosy treatment and a giant in many other ways. His life story intersects with other fascinating individuals such as W.G. Grace, the famous cricketer, Mahatma Gandi, Eric Liddell, (of "Chariots of Fire" fame), and Paul Brand.

He contributed much to the advancement of leprosy treatment but showed genuine compassion by physical contact with sufferers. I saw the human side of this man also, in the holidays we spent with him and his wife, experiencing his phenomenal ability to eat quantities of raw chillies. He ate green chillies as initiation into the "Chilli Club". Membership only one at the last count.

I was able to visit and spend time with him, when grieving over the sudden loss of his wife. His grief and despair took him almost over the edge of the cliff. But his strong faith in a time of grief and distress enabled him to keep going. Reading Psalm 73.2. gave me the title for this book.

"As for me, I came so close to the edge of the cliff."

There are plenty of books on leprosy including some that Bob was responsible for. His full list of published books (as well as numerous articles) is impressive -
- *Leprosy in India: a Survey.* London: World Dominion Press, 1927.
- *Leprosy in Europe: the Middle and Near East and Africa.* London: World Dominion Press, 1928.

- *Leprosy in the Far East.* London: World Dominion Press, 1929.
- *A Practical Textbook of Leprosy* with a foreword by George R. McRoberts. London: Oxford University Press, 1947.
- Cochrane, R G and T Frank Davey, *Leprosy in Theory and Practice.* Bristol: John Wright, 1959.
- Also *Biblical Leprosy: A Suggested Interpretation.* Great Britain: Tyndale Press, 1961.

Before my marriage I worked as a nurse. During my training, I saw a film about leprosy work. I found the images of the patients quite horrifying and made a mental resolution NEVER to get involved in leprosy treatment.

But God had other plans for my life. I married 'into leprosy'. My husband Ian and I served with The Leprosy Mission (earlier known as the Mission to Lepers) in India and Bangladesh. Robert was an expert in the field and his son Ian decided to follow that branch of medicine also, as his life's work. After more than 35 years in leprosy work with Ian, we retired to the U.K. Retirement, or as I prefer to call it – re-tyrement, ready for further service, presented new challenges.

I read, with great interest, biographies of other Christian leprosy workers. Then the seed thought came - why not the story of Robert Cochrane? He had made a big contribution to the progress in care and treatment of this disease. There seemed to be a gap in the history of leprosy which needed filling, and I felt I should try to fill it.

So with a leprosy background, the desire that his contribution should be recorded became important. This led to many visits to interesting people who knew him, worked with him or benefitted from his skills in treatment. I corresponded with others I could not visit. I also had the benefit of access to archives and libraries. I had embarked on a fascinating but daunting project. Places around the globe he had visited became more than a pin point on the map. Stories of people emerged that became part of his life and now mine. The key to all his activities was inspired by his strong Christian faith. This was the thread which ran through all of his varied

6

experiences and sustained him in so many difficulties. Finally I put a rough draft together of all the gathered material. But how to proceed and where to find the editor and publisher I had no idea.

The Leprosy Mission International had been helpful in providing much material from its archives. Now the key to open the next door also came from there. I was asked to provide a list of books in my possession which might be of interest for the library at Headquarters. Compiling this list I came to "I will lie down in peace" by Usha Jesudasan. After re-reading this I decided to try and contact her, for she seemed the ideal person to help me bring this daunting task to a successful conclusion. So it was again, God answered my prayers for help. But God had other plans. Usha is now with the Lord. I am indebted to others along the way, and now to John Whiteley for his invaluable help to edit all the material.

It is my hope and prayer that you will find this life story as fascinating and challenging as its preparation has been for me.

Marion G. Cochrane, M. B. E.

CHAPTER 1

A ROUGH START

" Their eyes are blue, their eyes are blue,

Hence earth lacks dew,

Earth lacks dew."

A little group of women, dressed in flowing robes and bare feet, walked behind Grace Cochrane chanting this song. Every time she heard these words, her heart froze a little. Grace had proudly shown off her beloved little twin babies - Robert and Thomas, both of whom had bright blue eyes, to the village women. At first, the babies were smiled and gooed at, but recently they were greeted with cold, dark stares and this toneless, frightening chanting. The words were cruel and foretold a terrible danger.

Grace and Dr.Thomas Cochrane had come to Chaoyang, in Eastern Mongolia, to serve with the London Missionary Society. As the medical work grew, another couple, Mr. and Mrs. Liddell, joined them to give the spiritual side of the work a boost. Grace and Thomas lived a very simple and almost primitive life without all the comfortable conveniences of a western home, but being accepted by the local people and helping them made life happy and meaningful for them.

Much had changed in the little town of Chaoyang, where Grace and Thomas ran a small clinic for the people living there. At first, they were welcomed and the local people were happy and grateful to have them around. They brought their sick children and elders to the young doctor and were thankful when their children or wives or parents did not die. Then slowly, things began to change. A famine swept through the country. There was hardly anything available in the markets. Children were getting hungrier and thinner every day. Then came the dreadful drought when water became scarce. Famine and drought brought much suffering to people who already had such a hard life. The local people whose minds were ruled by superstition and fear of misfortune, now saw the missionaries as the reason for all their troubles. They blamed the famine, the drought, sickness and all the other ills that befell them on the little blue-eyed, white children of the missionaries.

As the situation became tense, the chanting too increased with palpable anger, loudness and hostility. Relationships with the local people became more and more difficult. It did not seem wise to stay on in the midst of the quietly growing anger and seething hatred. They decided that the two wives and the three little boys would leave quietly with Mr. Liddell, who would escort them to the railhead, from where they could proceed to the coast. With great difficulty and secrecy, a cart was obtained and packed. Thick padded quilts were arranged in the cart to buffer the bumps and jolts of the rough roads. Bags and boxes were placed on the floor of the cart. In the dead of night, when everything was silent, the family crept out of the house. When everyone had boarded, the cart moved slowly. Dust flew from the wooden wheels as they turned round, their creaking making loud disturbing noises that cut into the silent night. The road was a dirt track with pot holes and stones and dips along the way. The mules which pulled the cart were used to this kind of road and moved slowly and effortlessly. The driver, annoyed at this sleepy pace, urged them on faster. Hearing the familiar command, the mules trotted faster, tossing the occupants in all directions. At one point, the cart was stopped by Boxer soldiers. The driver refused to allow his precious cargo to be captured and argued he must be killed first as he raced away, taking Grace and the boys to safety.

Thomas meanwhile returned to the house to continue his work. It soon became clear that his presence made it difficult and dangerous for the Chinese Christian staff to work and live normally in the community. Anti-foreigner feelings were intense as the Boxer rebellion spread, and Chinese Christians too were included in the hatred as they now belonged, it was deemed, to a foreign religion. So one night, Thomas quietly mounted his horse and just rode away, skirting towns, possible road blocks and known brigand areas.

Grace and the boys reached the station and Thomas too arrived safely. They embraced each other with great joy as they boarded the train to Shanghai. They were not completely out of danger and tensions remained high until they reached Shanghai on the coast. Here, Thomas became very ill with malaria and could not travel. Rather than have his family delay the trip and remain in danger, he sent them back home to England without him, and sailed as soon as he was fit to travel.

The voyage home took months and it was both hard and healing. Hard, as Grace had to manage three little boys on her own on a rocking ship, with few facilities; and healing, as it gave both her and Thomas when he travelled, time and distance away from the danger they had been in for some time. Their nerves were shattered by the growing hatred and the secrecy of the dangerous journey and not knowing if the other would make it to safety. The long journey was a time when their tired souls were quietly refreshed and restored by the sound of the waves and by reflection under the stars at night.

In Scotland, as the family finally gathered, there was great joy. The boys were overjoyed to see their father, and Grace was relieved that the long separation was at last over. Together they read Psalm 91, which begins,

"He who dwells in the shelter of the Most High will rest in the shadow of the

Almighty."

This was to become the Cochrane family Psalm.

So began the amazingly adventurous life of blue-eyed, fair-haired Robert Cochrane. Robert knew from a very young age that God had preserved him from the perils of long rough road travel, bandits, brigands, Boxers and the wrath of local peasants who thought the foreign devils responsible for their drought and resulting deprivation.

See Plate 1 Photo of the 3 boys Thomas, Edgar and Robert.

RETURN TO CHINA

By the end of 1901, it seemed safe to return, so the family, with four year old Edgar, and the twins, Robert and Thomas who were two years old, went back to Peking in China, and not to Outer Mongolia where they were before. Peking, in 1901, was a huge heap of rubbish and rubble after the Boxer Rising. On arrival in Peking, the Cochranes found that everything was a monotonous grey or black; ashes and fallen brick. Thomas stood and looked around sadly at the ruins of the hospital established by the London Missionary Society. The heap of grey bricks of which it was once built bore eloquent evidence of the hatred for the Westerner. Standing on the ruins, he prayed that he might be able to influence the throne of China somehow.

Thomas's dream was to train Chinese doctors who would look after their own countrymen and women. He worked tirelessly to this end and his prayer was answered when the Chinese Empress Dowager, once an enemy, now officially recognised the Peking Medical College and gave a substantial gift towards its rebuilding. Funds came too from China's Reparation to the Great Powers following the uprising.

While Thomas was busy rebuilding the hospital, Grace, who herself was a trained nurse, was busy in the home caring for Edgar, Robert (Bob) and Thomas (Tom). She was the glue that held the family together. Thomas's work often took him away from home and the boys missed him dearly. Robert, in later life, wrote of Grace, "It was she who in days of danger and peril ... shared my father's life. It was she who in later years, during intervals when the head of the family was away, kept the lamp of faith burning bright at the family altar." ('The Doctor and the Dragon' by Margaret Aitchison, p 48.)

In addition, Robert recalls in his C. V. - "My early education was undertaken by my Mother." After about two years of living in cramped, Chinese quarters, the family moved into one of the three houses in the L.M.S. compound where the house was much larger. The compound had an artesian well and a tennis court. Water still had to be carried upstairs to the bathrooms in buckets, but at least they had clean drinking water. Provisions still had to be brought out from England.

Robert's twin brother Tom wrote of the Peking years,

"Our standard of living was such as to be found amongst a well-established professional class of the Edwardian era at home. . . but there was always the threat of disease - smallpox, epidemics of cholera, typhoid, typhus, intestinal fevers, malaria, tropical sprue as well as the diseases occurring at home. The mortality and morbidity rate amongst missionaries was high and mother kept an eagle eye on hygiene. We had no nurse maid, mother took care of her children herself and this no doubt accounted for our good health. The climate was extreme, 110 degrees Fahrenheit in summer and probably minus 20 degrees Fahrenheit in winter.

When Edgar was about seven he went to boarding school in Tiensin, which he hated. American parents there complained that their children spoke with a Scottish accent. Bob and I did not go to school until we returned from China and were by then nine years old. We did have some instruction from Mother but we were about a year behind.

Father was a workaholic and remained at work when all the other Europeans were on vacation. He used to come out to the hills, which were a day's journey, for two or three days at a time. We returned from the hills in early autumn." (The Doctor and the Dragon, P128)

All three boys became doctors in different fields of medicine, but only Bob became world famous (or infamous with his total disregard for what was deemed a very infectious disease), with a personal letter of commendation from the President of the USA.

CHAPTER 2

EDUCATION IN ENGLAND

The three boys all started at a school established in 1842 for the sons of missionaries in Blackheath, London on September 15th 1908. This must have been a very difficult day for all the family and particularly for Grace, parting with all the boys at once, leaving them in England when they returned once more to China. Grace was not the only one to find the separation from the three boys very difficult. After reading of the struggle Abraham went through trying to obey God's instruction, Thomas recorded in his diary, "In thy seed shall all the nations of the earth be blessed, because thou hast obeyed my voice". He quoted Genesis 22.18 and added, "This means My Father, that Thou wilt make it up to my three boys." (Quoted from The Doctor and the Dragon page 129).

Edgar was now 11 and the twins were 9 years old.

See Plate 2 Photo Robert, Edgar and Thomas at Hither Green.

Mr. and Mrs. Liddell's two sons, Rob and Eric were admitted to the school the day before on 14th September 1908.

It is likely that the boys attended a lantern lecture during their first term on 6th November 1908 entitled 'China' by Rev. A. E. Claxton, who was a missionary there.

In June 1909 Bob contracted Scarlet Fever, and Thomas contracted diphtheria. Both were taken to the hospital, and the school closed early for the summer holidays. Prize Day had to be postponed. Diphtheria, then Measles and Pertussis (whooping cough) followed. All this at boarding school in England before he was twelve.

Bob also recalls in his C. V. "My repeated attempts to join the army were frustrated by my being rejected because of a heart condition which was probably due to a serious attack of diphtheria in 1909."

At the end of their second year at school in July 1911, Bob won a Merit Prize in Form 1, along with 3 other boys, one of whom was Eric Liddell. He enjoyed sport and there is a photo of him in the rugby team.

In January 1912 the school moved to much more pleasant premises in Mottingham, South East London where it still thrives under the name Eltham College. For the first time the boys had their own playing fields, better facilities and even a swimming bath. The school magazine of the time recorded that "it has been delightful to lie on the grass or to wander down the shady grove on a hot Sunday afternoon with a book or maybe a guinea pig under one's arm".

Dr. and Mrs. Cochrane were amongst several who contributed to the Prize Fund for Sports Day in 1912. The prizes purchased with this money included a pen-knife, an inkstand, a flash lamp, a pocket lens and water wings. Infectious diseases again struck the school in 1913 when measles, German Measles and Influenza caused the postponement of the Athletic Sports. Dr. Cochrane preached in the chapel on May 9[th.] Dr. Ernest Peill was seriously ill in Peking, and travelled home to Glasgow via Siberia. "He was fortunate to have the company and care of Dr. Cochrane as far as London."

By 1914 the numbers had increased to 111– 40 more than when the school moved to Eltham in January 1912. Later in the year this rose to 125.

Edgar was now a prefect and the twins in Form IV passed the Preliminary Cambridge Local Examinations. It was not all work though. Nine boys swam the maximum distance of one mile, and Bob was one of them, and this in a pool not heated. Perhaps this contributed to his always feeling the cold in later life!

The famous Cricketer W. G. Grace, now in his mid-sixties, lived near the school and brought a team to play the 1st XI, which must have stimulated interest in the game considerably.

The First World War did not disrupt the school as much as the Second World War, so sports, exams, societies and debates continued, but old boys began to appear in khaki uniforms, and of the 120 who served 34 were killed. The large plaque in the chapel honours their names.

One of the memories of all boarders is the writing letters home on a Sunday and this the boys did to their parents. We can only imagine what they wrote, but I am sure that the sporting events and achievements were written about and received with equal joy and pride, likewise the academic achievements - not so the illnesses and treatment of any misdemeanours!

Edgar left school at the end of 1914 and with Dr. and Mrs. Cochrane back in England the twins were able to attend school as day boys. What a joy it must have been to Grace to have them living with her once more after the years of separation and agonisingly long waits for letters to arrive by sea mail with news of their doings from school in the UK.

See Plate 3 Photo of Thomas and Robert as teenagers.

Progressing up the school and taking Junior Local Cambridge exams did not prevent the twins from enjoying sport, particularly rugby, when they both were in the 1st XV. Tom as a lightly built energetic wing forward, Bob as a slow, but hard working forward, who tackled well, went hard when he had the ball, and well deserved his place in the team but was rather fond of getting off-side.

The twins were both in the Cadet Corps, Tom being promoted to Lance Corporal, while Edgar sustained a shrapnel wound over the eye in the real war, from which he made a good recovery.

Later in 1916 he was again wounded by a sniper whilst crawling away with a wounded comrade on his back, but he was able to re-join his regiment after recovery. 1916-1917 season for the rugby 1st XV was more successful and Eric Liddell was in the team with Tom and Bob, and Rob Liddell was captain.

The twins also played in the match against Old Boys that year, with Tom playing very well, but with unfortunate results for Bob when "Muir made one of his characteristic charges through what he thought to be a scrum, but which in reality was Bob's head which was cut, proving Muir's to be the harder of the two!"

The prestigious Bayard prize for the boy who exerted the best influence in the school during the year, presented by Sir Alfred Pearce Gould, the eminent surgeon and Treasurer of the Baptist Missionary Society, went to Bob.

What a proud moment for the parents of the twins to be present, rather than thousands of miles away in China, and how their hearts must have again rejoiced that God's hand had protected the young family so that Edgar was serving his country and the twins had now grown up healthy and strong, finished their schooling with such accomplishments.

The prayer of Thomas after reading of Abraham in the Bible and adding in faith that his Heavenly Father would undertake for the three boys' needs and make them a blessing was being answered for their benefit and to strengthen his own faith for future events in the family.

(material obtained by courtesy of Eltham College Archives)

MEDICAL TRAINING

Bob went to Glasgow University which was near his Mother's native home in Scotland and where his father had trained. By this time his Father was in London after completing a World Survey of Leprosy for the Mission to Lepers. This was an amazingly informative survey of information meticulously collected from leprosy centres around the world, and for which the Mission was extremely grateful. In 1923 Thomas was a member of the Leprosy Mission Council and also on the Committee of BELRA (British Empire Leprosy Relief Association) as well as the Editor of World Dominion, a press he established to promote circulation of Christian news from around the world.

Bob qualified in 1924 with some commendation and then spent time at St. Bartholomew's Hospital, the London School of Hygiene and Tropical Medicine obtaining experience and an additional qualification before sailing for India the same year in October. Quite a full nine months!

See Plate 4 Photo Robert as a medical student.

THE INFLUENCE OF FAMILY GENES AND BACKGROUND

Dr. Thomas Cochrane spent many months, at the request of the Council of the Mission to engage in a World Survey of Leprosy.

"This he did with meticulous care to detail and in such a systematic way both filed and with a card index. Thus it is possible at once by reference to this file to obtain detailed and first hand information regarding leprosy in any given part of the world. In addition to the above, Dr. T Cochrane has gathered together very complete particulars regarding medical and general mission work. This enables leprosy work to be viewed in its proper standing in relation to the missionary enterprise as a whole. From this statement it will be seen how valuable the results of Dr. Cochrane's Survey are." (Quote from Mr. Grundy Acting Secretary. TLMI Archives).

So it was a God-given gift to Thomas that enabled him to use his medical skills and his diplomacy to obtain so much information from centres around the world, and assemble it in such a way that it was an extremely useful tool for reference and guidance. In his letter written from World Dominion at the end of 1923 he wrote to colleagues with great understanding of their particular situations, "I know only too well from actual experience how busy medical missionaries are, but I also know how keen they are to help in such inspiring and comprehensive plans as I have outlined. Your help will be greatly valued.

Fraternally yours,

Tho Cochrane."

In that same letter he acknowledges that the questionnaire was drawn up by the British Empire Leprosy Relief Association, revealing the fact that he regarded himself as a channel and in no way the instigator of the plan.

This was to be repeated by Bob with regard to record keeping and prodigious detailed work, his work focusing on examination of slides under the microscope in the laboratory from around the world, in his persistent thirst for knowledge concerning leprosy, linked with his great desire for the spread of the Gospel. His vision was worldwide and he believed as his Father had done concerning work in China, that "...it is a long and arduous campaign and a wide view and the most careful planning are necessary" (page 138 The Doctor and the Dragon).

CHAPTER 3

INDIA

In Bob's own words, "Even though I never was good at keeping a diary, I suppose one's early impressions become fixed in the mind.

I sailed for India with, I am sure, not little emotion, in October 1924 in the company of Mr. and Mrs. Anderson, at that time the then General Secretary of the Mission to Lepers (now The Leprosy Mission). He was the link between the founder of the Mission, Mr. Wellesley Bailey and the dawning of the new hope for those suffering from leprosy.

Human memory, however, is short and the present favourable outlook is often taken for granted, but in the early days leprosy was much more a disease to be hidden, a word whispered in the dark, lest it should be heard by others. In many ways leprosy was the forgotten disease. Except for a very few scientific workers such as H. W. Wade of the Philippines, Ernest Muir of Calcutta (now Kolkata), Marchoux of France, and Denney in the USA, leprosy had hardly entered seriously into the thinking of medical Men.

It is well therefore, to remind my readers of this, lest these times pass out of history without record, and the struggles and efforts to bring leprosy into a place of respectability be omitted from the present day leprosy story'". So wrote Bob in the 1960s.

The lack of effective treatment, the failure to appreciate the very early signs of the disease, the long stream of hopelessly crippled, blind and disconsolate men and women cursed by society, gradually dampened enthusiasm, and almost extinguished the flame of interest in those early days.

Just before and after the causative organism of leprosy was discovered by Dr Armauer Hanson in 1872 (publicly announced in 1874) the smouldering embers were kept from being completely smothered by a few faithful workers. By and large however, enthusiasm waned and the whole subject was side-tracked.

Also at this time from 1897, an American Presbyterian missionary, Dr. James McKean appealed to the authorities in Thailand for permission to establish a leprosy asylum on Koh Klang Island four kilometres south of Chiang Mai, to treat those with leprosy who were ostracised and outcast due to the stigma attached to the disease. Chaulmoogra oil had been used as a cure by Mouat, a British Surgeon in India. But this remedy was largely discarded, because of its nauseating properties when given by mouth.

The discovery of Mycobacterium Leprae by Professor Hansen suggested to Professor Koch to search for a similar organism in tuberculosis and M. Tuberculosa was isolated 14 years later, in 1886.

CHAULMOOGRA OIL

This had been the traditional treatment for leprosy in the Indian and Chinese pharmacopea for probably thousands of years. The origins of many indigenous remedies are buried in legend, folklore and traditional stories.

THE CALL

More from Bob's own words -

"Since the day when I, with the enthusiasm and zeal of youth, entered my life's work, many persons have asked me why I chose leprosy. I stand quite firmly on the faith of my Father's and make no excuse for claiming sincerely and reverently to be a committed Christian.

To sit by the side of a dying patient, dying from the effects of the disease and not to be able to raise a finger to help is a bitter experience. This was my lot in the days when advanced leprosy was indeed incurable. I well remember doing just this, when a patient of mine who was one of my greatest friends lay dying. The thought of this experience remains impressed vividly on my mind. Some may say, 'but you should not make such friends of patients.' Medicine brings great rewards but the friendly touch is the privilege of the dedicated doctor.

I vaguely remember as a boy in my teens, it may have been a sermon that started the trend of thought, it may have been some Biblical reference that turned my attention to the subject, it may have been the challenge that leprosy work offered. Whatever the motive, when my father shortly after I graduated said to me, 'The Mission to Lepers (now The Leprosy Mission) needs a doctor, are you interested?'

Without a sense of emotion, without a feeling of elation that at the thought that at last I could fulfil my heart's desire, I replied 'Yes'.

A man cannot dedicate his life to a set goal without a purpose, and in some measure an emotional reaction must always be present. While the acceptance of my first job seemed matter of fact enough there remained a deep satisfaction that I had entered on a life's work which subconsciously had been my desire ever since the day when I dreamt, not knowing its significance, that I found a cure for leprosy.

In those days when I first set out on my life's work the voyage took 3 weeks. Today forty two years later (in 1962) the time has only been slightly reduced to two weeks from Southampton to Bombay. The P. and O. boat anchored off shore before it was allowed to dock. To me the sights and smells of the East came as a refreshment of memory. The only difference was the colour of the skin of the people, not the sallow tint of the Mongolian, but the variegated colouring of the masses of the people from the light coloured figure of the Parsee to the dark almost black skin of the South Indian and those of what man has deemed the outcaste but what Gandhiji aptly called "the Harijan"- a word almost misused today, for to Gandhiji they were indeed the people of God. Did not our Lord call such people his friends?

Bombay (known now as Mumbai) as now, was then a fascinating city. Varied as cities of the east are, relics of ancient civilisation, in the days when Britain was but a land of primitive, and in many ways, uncivilised and uncouth barbarians.

It was the evening hour that left an indelible mark on an impressionable youth, for stretched out all along the side walks were men wrapped round in what looked like shrouds, only to find that they were sleeping figures, either to escape the heat of indoors or the only place they could call home.

The shout of the gariwaller, (cart driver or rickshaw puller) the street cries, the smells and noises made an amalgam of strange attractiveness. I loved every moment of my introduction to India, a land of mystery and challenge, of poverty and wealth, of spirituality and darkness, a land which I came to love as if it were my own native land, a land which is today closer to my heart than any other and I can join reverently and sincerely in the patriotic shout, 'Jai Hind'.

On arrival at Ballards Pier in Bombay we were met by Donald Miller, the Secretary for India for The Mission to Lepers (now the Leprosy Mission). Mr. Miller sorted the details of our baggages etc. and we went to a missionary home where we stayed for the few days we were in Bombay. It was here I had my first experience of a jutka, the horse drawn vehicle, a mixture of a hansom cab and a carriage.

There were 2 Leprosy Homes in the Bombay Presidency (now called the State of Maharashtra), and to reach them one had to cross the bay by a ferry. I remember, while the first sight of a leprosy patient brought no conscious feeling of revulsion or fear, except for the fact that when I handled the patients, the skin of my hands felt strange, not an itchiness but a kind of uneasiness which made me wash my hands with extra care. Since those days I have become possibly too careless, but after 44 years of working in intimate contact with leprosy, I believe that if anybody has immunity I have it in a big way. I hope that I handled patients then and now not with the carelessness of which my friends accused me, but with a nonchalance prompted by the thought that to touch patients with leprosy is a necessity, to show sympathy for what I then called, and never would call today 'lepers' was essential. There is no better way to convey human understanding and affection than by the sympathetic touch.

I did not appreciate in those days that the majority of the human race could not get leprosy, no matter how they tried. The whole story of genetics in leprosy is a fascinating one, and if studied might give the answer to the question why some appear easily to acquire the infection whereas others, whatever they do, appear to have a built in immunity. If leprosy had been as contagious a disease as many of my friends in those days thought it was, I should have been infected long ago for I worked with the patients in the closest contact. There is a malady however, that which I believe is completely and utterly incurable, and this is called 'lepraphobia'" – the fear of leprosy.

In spite of four decades and more leprosy work, or perhaps because of it, the whole subject has been divorced from the mainstream of Medicine. This lack of emphasis of leprosy in relation to medicine and its separateness, has been exaggerated and is detrimental both to the speciality and to medicine as a whole. Even in the diseases such as tuberculosis, malignant diseases and such chronic conditions as rheumatoid arthritis, this separation from the mainstream of medicine is not so marked and does not adversely affect the outlook of the general public. Chronic and in some ways more disastrous conditions such as rheumatoid arthritis and lupus vulgaris, do not give rise to the same ostracism and fear even though they are in many ways as disfiguring and crippling as leprosy. Nevertheless, in spite of the handicap due to the emotional motives placed on leprosy, there have been great advances in the scientific study of the disease and a notable new era has dawned with corresponding fascinating and interesting results . Unfortunately however, because of ancient prejudices, fairy tales and folklore, because of the mistaken Biblical references, clinical leprosy is still frequently looked upon as a disease not really worthy of the attention of the best minds. There are of course some notable exceptions, but by and large the specialty of leprosy has not been integrated into medicine or adequately taught in the major medical schools. Today matters are better, but still leprosy is too often a passing reference in the lecture room and not taken seriously even though millions suffer from this age long affliction."

(written by Bob Cochrane in the 1960s)

WHAT IS IT ?

If you are still with me on this journey, you are probably asking, "but *what is* leprosy? Why is it such a hated disease and why is there not more known about it in this modern scientific age?"

This book is not intended to teach about the disease but I feel sure that some readers will be asking what it is and how it is manifest. So as simply as I can put it in a nutshell, as we used to do for awareness purposes:-

It is a disease that affects the skin and certain nerves of the body.

It is caused by a germ.

Its incubation period can be as much as 18 years.

It is not hereditary but it is estimated that 97% of the population are fortunate to have immunity, the remaining 3% are not.

It is only mildly infectious and in the Guinness Book of Records as the least contagious of all contagious diseases.

Leprosy is not a spectacular disease as it starts with a small spot.

Its first signs can often be a patch on the skin – reddish on pale skin and peanut butter colour on the dark skin.

The patch has less feeling, less colour, less hair and tends to be dry, but does not itch. There may be other signs such as swollen ear lobes, tingling or weakness in the fingers or toes.

It is curable and early treatment prevents deformity.

But please remember that you are most likely to be in that fortunate 95 - 97% of the population so don't go running in panic mode to the doctor if you think you have the disease, after reading this!

A healthy life style with good balanced diet, exercise and rest go a long way towards prevention of any infection, including leprosy. The symptoms are very insidious. Any lack of feeling may be due to a previous injury or surgery.

This has been the experience of many a person who has been associated with leprosy patients and then fear they themselves have been infected, only to find on examination that there was a history of injury or a knee operation being the cause. Now back to the story.

CHAPTER 4

PURULIA AND BANKURA

As Medical Secretary for the Mission to Lepers Bob visited Purulia, established as an Ashram (shelter) in 1888, and Bankura, both in West Bengal. The increasing number of patients prompted the need for more buildings in Purulia.

Buildings were constructed for Wards, an out patients Treatment Block and a large church, called appropriately The Church of the Good Samaritan.

By February the next year (1925) Bob had visited Purulia and Bankura in West Bengal where the latter was establishing a Medical School and the former could benefit from a doctor being posted there.

It was already becoming clear that Bob had a discerning eye for observing current situations and being able to focus on the direction needed for developing and improving the standard of the work already established.

During the following ten weeks there were visits to nine different centres involving considerable travel and by April 10th 1925 he was travelling to Dichpalli in Central Provinces (now called Andhra Pradesh). Much of the travel would have been on Indian trains with some local form of transport to reach the various centres from the train stations, always tucked discreetly some distance from the centre of towns.

Train journeys would invariably start late at night and arrive very early in the morning or even in the middle of the night. Fortunately Bob was able to sleep anywhere and mostly the guard would come and notify that the next station was the one required, banging loudly on the door of the sleeper compartment waking all the occupants inside regardless of their destination. In any case the lights would go on

27

and the departing passenger assemble and lock luggage and make sure nothing was left behind, under the pillow, in the fold by the wall when the berth was lowered for sleeping, or under the berth on the gritty floor. Local transport may have been any of the following depending on the area and the distance from the station to the Institution - a bullock cart with wooden wheels and no rubber tyres, a variety of either horse drawn carts known as Jodkas or man pulled rickshaws. Some of the larger centres may well have boasted a car which would suffer badly with the potholes of unmade tracks and lack of maintenance.

The letters make no mention of the difficulties or inconveniences of travel which were accepted as part of life in the East and not worthy of mention when there was so much of greater importance to record and report. There was a need for a training centre, with Purulia being suggested as a good possibility. Staff changes are mentioned as well as the fact that the new doctor showed considerable hesitancy when asked to dress ulcers. The need for expatriate doctors at the major centres was also expressed.

We have to remember that much less was known about the disease then and its possible infection which would account somewhat for the reticence. Indeed the first encounter with patients can be daunting.

Bob noted that outpatient work needed to be developed as well as better organised medical care of the in-patients on the wards. He linked the prolonged treatment now being given by injections with chaulmoogra oil as an opportunity to give these men the Gospel for a prolonged period also, seeing the work as a holistic effort for the patients to receive physical and spiritual care.

He was also full of praise for work being done in one centre, which was nothing short of excellent considering the grossly inadequate staff. Whilst there he performed several operations including cataract, demonstration of ulcer care and some minor operations.

At the end of his visit he was embarrassed to be presented with a small gold cross which an elderly patient trembling with age and nervousness, pinned to his shirt, quite without the knowledge of the superintendent. "You can well understand with what feelings of unworthiness and gratitude I received this token of their gratitude and love." So began a deep and precious relationship with leprosy patients which would continue for many years to come with a steady flow of such gifts as he gave himself to their treatment and continued to show them he cared deeply for their every need by giving them his time and full attention.

Early in 1925 the suggestions for the expansion and development of the work in Purulia were progressing through the various stages of committees and Council meetings.

The need for a separate home for healthy girls (whose parents had leprosy) was approved, as was accommodation for two lady workers from England, new wards and a store room for grain.

The Government of India were approached for a grant towards all this building expense. Letters flowed between Bob and the General Secretary now in Hong Kong, advocating that Bob plan a trip to China and meet one Professor in Peking. Disappointingly the political unrest meant that the longed for visit to the land of his birth did not materialise for Bob.

There was an admonition to not work too hard and take some time off for rest before leaving for the Far East. Another letter requested advice on the present and future policy of the Mission centred round indicators such as new centres needed, which ones to develop, and the strengthening of the evangelistic work of the Mission alongside the medical development.

A request was made that if it appeared that a centre was grossly understaffed this may be mentioned in the report but not to the staff of the institution who may request vastly increased budgets, (not possible).

INDIAN TOUR

Visits were made to seventeen centres and reports of each sent back to the Head Office in London, or to the staging post on the extensive travels, such as Hong Kong, or Melbourne to keep abreast of the reports on visits, and to keep the leaders of the mission well informed.

The second half of 1925 saw plans for a further eighteen centres to be visited and reported on in India before embarking on a tour further East.

There was great unity of purpose between the two men, one the more senior administrator and the other the young medical hothead so full of zeal and enthusiasm, totally committed to the task in hand and relishing the thought of developing the work and extending its influence. They both concurred that a centre of excellence should be established in each province with direction by a European doctor, where treatment would be given and training given so that other similar centres could be established, followed later by the training of national doctors as well.

Their ideas so in unison, formulated when they were far apart indicates the power of prayer as they committed their lives and their work to God's purposes, creating a wonderful unity of purpose.

Creating centres of excellence was to be a recurring theme for Dr. Paul Brand many years later.

POSSIBLE CHANGE OF PLAN

By October 1925 there was a suggestion that Bob return to England earlier so that discussions could be held about formulating Mission Policy for work in India which appeared to be more pressing than visiting other countries such as the Philippines. Nevertheless a visit to Burma, Thailand, Singapore and Malaya, Borneo and via India before proceeding to England was suggested.

There was also the quality of a Statesman emerging, just as his father Thomas had done in China very early in the 1900s in Peking.

CALCUTTA SCHOOL OF TROPICAL MEDICINE.

As if the arduous travel and work of the visiting as Secretary for Medical Work was not sufficient, time was made to write about concern for the need of an additional research worker at the Calcutta School of Tropical Medicine and this was discussed with Dr. Thomas Cochrane now in London.

CORRESPONDENCE WITH MISSION TO LEPERS.

It was the practice to number letters and this made referrals to them easier and also to note if any letters were lost in the post, as did happen sometimes. The flow of reports was appreciated in London and also that there had been opportunities to address public meetings in various places, one of which was in Bangkok in the presence of Princes and Nobility.

The amusing comment followed to the effect that it was hoped it was not necessary to purchase a larger sized topee the next day, in consequence!

Personal concerns are not overlooked as there was mention in a letter in February 1926 of "your dear Mother's lying so seriously ill. We all rejoice that she is now in a convalescent stage, after a very anxious time for your Father. We had you in very prayerful remembrance and especially your Mother". (TLMI Archives)

THE PURULIA SCENE.

The area for the work was situated a couple of miles from the centre of the town and reached by rickshaw over unmade roads with potholes worn deeper by the bullock cart wheels carrying loads of rice, bamboo, earth from building sites and mud bricks to them, water in drought and rice paddy at harvest time also many other supplies required by the local population.

The approach road was planted with trees which gave welcome shade in the hot sun to those walking down to the Out Patients Department or hoping for admission, and too poor to pay for any transport or shunned by the rickshaw pullers due to the obvious signs of the disease or foul smelling ulcers concealed under dirty rags.

At the start of the rains the land would be ploughed by teams of bullocks and once the fields were flooded the precious rice seedlings would be transplanted with singing as the rows of workers stood ankle deep in the mud with bunches of seedlings. The crop would have grown since the monsoon rainy season from June to August. But after the rice harvest the fields were for months dry and the earth baked and cracked awaiting the next monsoon. Lack of water and irrigation made the fields a dust bowl for months on end, and in March when the hot winds blew (known as the loo winds) the dust would penetrate closed doors and windows and settle in thick layers on every horizontal surface. At the entrance to the hospital stood a large pipal tree and people could find welcome shelter in the shade of its generous branches. After the long hot walk, the pipal tree gave welcome shade. Dr. George Archer treated the patients with great care and dedication, as an expression of his strong faith.

In the stifling heat patients would prefer to sit outside to benefit from any little breeze and Bob certainly said that he used to prefer to operate under a tree than inside the building, partly because of the heat and partly because of the foul smell from some of the ulcers. It has to be admitted that entering a hospital ward and finding the beds all empty, while the occupants sit on the steps outside or worse still to be standing, not helping to heal their ulcers at all, is a strange experience to the medical eye.

By mid 1925 plans for the tour of the Far East were made and approved giving freedom to alter plans at his own discretion according to the circumstances, not being able to consult with quick replies as is possible today. Cables were much used to send urgent instructions and information, and the art of briefing with the minimum of words mastered, to keep down the cost.

CHAPTER 5

BACK TO INDIA

By 1928 Bob and Ivy had made their home in Bankura, West Bengal, and according to an official visitor they both looked very well and happy. Bob being teased about his increasing weight but taken with his usual good humour, an oft quoted symptom of newly wed husbands.

'Mrs. Cochrane is very happy and studying Bengali.' When this was written she must have been pregnant with her first child (Cameron) who was born in Kalimpong on September 5th that year.

Bob took to the rigours of travel in India like a duck to water, but not so Ivy. Like other missionary wives she was learning Bengali to enable her to speak to local people, patients and staff.

The medical work there was brought up to the standard deemed right by Bob, and no doubt the patients appreciated the additional care taken by Ivy when visiting and practising her Bengali.

Their presence would have been a great stimulus to the staff in their work and the patients in their renewed hope of improvement if not cure. The new treatment with the painful injections of chaulmoogra oil could be faced with greater courage when supported by the Doctor and his wife plus the team of faithful national workers.

The need for meticulous records which were the hallmark of Bob's careful work over the years, was instilled to every member of staff, for nothing slipshod was good enough for the patients under his care. Staff would soon realise that careless work in this area was rewarded with a reprimand from their chief, delivered firmly, courteously, not in front of the patient or other staff.

Mr. Miller with his keen perception observed that the meagre knowledge of the language was a problem for the Superintendent, but that difficulty should gradually disappear. Bob's interest in people, and his specially kindly way should be a help to the Superintendent.

During 1928 correspondence mentioned needs of various mission homes and illness of staff for prayer. Constant tiring travel meant there was little time for report writing, let alone time with his pregnant wife. Then when she was delivered in September, a quick trip to the hills to see her and their first born son, Cameron, involved a journey of 2 nights in the train to reach the northern hills.

The pressing needs urged him on and in the days of having to dictate letters and reports to a secretary, were time consuming without all the modern technology, other than shorthand typists and carbon copies in the typewriter using foolscap paper. Diligent secretaries worked hard to keep up with the flow of frequent correspondence between hospitals, Indian office officials and the Head office in London. Considering the hazards of sea mail and the lengthy rail journeys from the Indian ports, it is amazing that the flow of news was so regular and prompt. Numbering of letters soon alerted the recipient if one was missing, and a repeat was requested.

The pattern of late nights and early mornings to spend time in Bible reading and prayer were set in stone – the corner stone of his faith in Jesus as Lord.

The General Secretary was gratified that Bob was also able to report on the increase in the efficiency of the medical standard at Purulia.

In mid 1928 a suggestion was made to hold a leprosy conference in or near Singapore so that workers in Asia and the Far East could meet, but the suggestion was not received with enthusiasm by the authorities at that time. So it is interesting that in later years conferences were held in different parts of the world enabling those working in the field to attend and share their experience and exchange valuable expertise with others for their mutual benefit. It was not until 1933 that a conference was held in Calcutta.

The Secretary for India shared with the Head Office his concern about outpatients at Bankura being irregular with their attendance, which would hamper their progress towards healing. But he also expressed the confidence that Bob's intensive work would do much to raise the standard of the total work of the place, including motivation for better attendance.

CHAPTER 6

A NEW APPOINTMENT - TIME IN UK.

In 1929 Bob became the General Secretary for BELRA (British Empire Leprosy Association).

Based in England he travelled extensively to Africa and the West Indies, until 1935. Writing reports on his findings during these visits, he also wrote :-

PROGRESS IN TREATMENT FOR LEPROSY, 1924 – 1934.

This is not the place to detail the history of the development of leprosy prevention. Sufficient is it to say that, as a result of the medical work of the past ten years, the disease is understood very much better and also what cannot be done is better appreciated. Institutional work must ever be in the forefront, and therefore, the Mission's sphere of usefulness will tend to increase. I have witnessed the enormous change in the development of medical treatment in our institutions since 1924, when the new hope was beginning to dawn. At that time the cases in our homes were such that little could be done for them; yet, even then the devoted band of workers accomplished that which seemed almost humanly impossible. Today along with the derelicts who will ever be a care for those with Christian compassion, are patients in the earlier stages presenting themselves for treatment, and it is in these cases that the full benefit is seen. It is possible however, to alleviate lepra–fever, which in many instances can be controlled, and the terrible ravages produced by advanced ulceration can be to a very large extent alleviated.

Dr. Ernest Muir was based at the Calcutta School of Tropical Medicine, he succeeded Sir Leonard Rogers and was equally enthusiastic in his interest about leprosy and a possible cure with chaulmoogra oil. It would arrest leprosy and in many cases would cure it. After decades of prayer and hard work it seemed that at last asylums and

37

refuges might be transformed into real hospitals offering effective treatment and perhaps discharging people free of the disease that had wrecked their lives.

But if the medical researchers had found a remedy it was not so easy to find the chaulmoogra fruit. True the trees grew in south west India, Myanmar, Thailand and Indo-China. But Muir had to find out where they could be reached. They ripened in the middle of the monsoon season – and the rains made the forests almost impassable. One of the most bizarre episodes in the fight against leprosy must surely be the struggle of the American botanist, Joseph Bock and Medical School Professor, Ernest Muir, hacking their way through the rainforests of India and South East Asia searching for the best chaulmoogra fruit available! That they found it at last in Kerala, South India is a tribute to determined courage as well as scientific knowledge.' (page 62 of Caring comes first – The Leprosy Mission Story by Cyril Davey.)

FAMILY EVENT

By 1930 Ivy with Cameron now 2 years old was living in Orpington, Kent while Bob continued his worldwide travels. In May he was visiting Turkey and Ivy heard of a plane crash in that country , fearing for her husband's safety, went into premature labour and Ian was born, a good six weeks early. It would be many years before the health problem caused by that precipitous birth would be discovered.

In 1936 Bob was interviewed by one Maurice Whitlow and it is recorded on Page 243 of "Great Thoughts: The Search For A Cure Of Leprosy"
"Dr. Cochrane is as yet only a comparatively young man. Less than a dozen years ago he took his qualifying examinations, and set out on what has since been the consuming passion of his life. He had a "call" in those days to devote himself to the care, and if possible the cure, of the leper.

First of all he went to India to co-operate with the Mission to Lepers. There had been

38

an unavoidable marking time period in leprosy research work since the end of the nineteenth century.

The re-discovery of chaulmoogra oil in India marked a further step in the conquest of this mysterious affliction. This oil had been known to Indians for thousands of years, and its rediscovery and adaption to skilled medicinal purposes by Sir Leonard Rogers in India and Dr. Heiser in the Philippines was a matter of first class importance.

As Medical Secretary to the British Empire Leprosy Association, Dr. Cochrane has visited parts of Africa, the West Indies, India and Ceylon (now Sri Lanka). In all these places he has made suggestions, through his Committee to the Government. "Nevertheless, among great numbers of people, even in administrative circles, the apathy is terrible." Said the doctor to me.

"You must remember that leprosy is not a dramatic disease, like cholera or malaria, sweeping thousands suddenly to death. Moreover it does not give way before any specific remedy, as malaria does to quinine. It is no part of the Association's work or plan to consider leprosy to the exclusion of other diseases. As it is not a spectacular disease, and begins with a small spot on the body, it can easily be hidden and not be discovered until the victim is in a serious condition. Not long ago we used to speak of the number of lepers in the ratio of victims to 100,000 of the population of a known infected area. Now there are countries in the Empire where we speak of the number of known lepers per hundred of the population."

See Plate 5 Photo Robert as a doctor (by Messrs Elliot and Fry Ltd).

THE INTERNATIONAL LEPROSY CONGRESS
In 1938 the International Leprosy Congress met in Cairo, Egypt. There had been earlier meetings of those doctors interested in sharing their news and views on the

fascinating disease. In 1897 there had been a meeting in Berlin, Germany where there was division about its contagion and possibly being hereditary. However these doctors were not going to let any such division obstruct their quest for more knowledge, rather it was a spur to further activity and meeting again in 1902, in Bergen, Norway, where there was still much work going on with patients in that country. The intense work of Dr. Armauer Hanson had led to his discovery of the leprosy bacillus under his microscope in 1873.

After the cause of the disease had been found, the desire to find a cure increased the motivation of those engrossed in the task.

Another meeting was convened in Strasbourg in 1923, but in 1931, when the experts again met in Manilla, The Philippines, it was decided to establish the meeting as an official body as numbers of participants increased and the need to share knowledge more vital. Many were now able to share their own personal experience and wisdom from many countries, with the variations of the disease which emerged from the different countries represented. So it became the first International Leprosy Congress.

The ramifications of this organisation were to have a great impact in future years, with the International Journal of Leprosy publishing articles written specifically for it and focusing on the many aspects which were being investigated and researched.

On the reverse side of the dinner menu of the 1938 Cairo congress there are seven signatures of prominent delegates, doctors who shared the same table and recorded their names.

The names include H. de Souza, E. Muir, H. W. Wade, John Lowe, Victor Heiser, Perry Burgess and last, Robt. G. Cochrane.

See Plate 5 Photo Robert as a doctor.

As World War 2 engulfed Europe and much of the East as well, it was to be ten years before the next International Leprosy Congress could meet and discuss the latest momentous developments. Sadly political unrest and upheavals let alone full scale wars, tribal, national and international continue to restrict the progress towards a world without leprosy.

The slogan of Dr. K. Ramanujam placed on all his envelopes was "And now on to a world without leprosy".

This is still appropriate in the 21st century as the battle still needs to be waged against this scourge which has baffled us for centuries and has caused so much grief, sorrow and suffering. There may be drugs to kill the leprosy germ, but still the battle needs to be won on other fronts, such as deformity and the stigma still attached to the disease in many parts of the world, mainly due to fear and ignorance.

CHAPTER 7

THE INVITATION

The Church of Scotland staffed and managed the Leprosy Centre at Tirumani, Near Chingleput, Madras Presidency, South India.

Its full title was Lady Willingdon Leprosy Sanatorium.

The work went on under Bob's leadership, after he accepted their invitation, which meant leaving The Mission to Lepers, but with a dedicated team of staff and patients, he would emphasise.

See Plate 10 photo of Robert doing ulcer round at Chingleput.
See Plate 12 photo of Dr Ramanujam co-worker who called him "guru".

This work continued while World War 2 raged in Europe. The General Secretary and his wife returned to England by ship. Their story is told in a little book entitled "A Ship, a Ship" written by Mr. A. D. Miller.

Bob wrote to him at the mission head office in London, in August 1942.
"My dear Donald,
As soon as we heard that you had been torpedoed I wrote to the Bible House Capetown. You and your wife have been much in our prayers. My article in World Dominion (His Father's Press) will give you some idea of the developments here. I am now Physician in charge of the Leprosy Department at the General Hospital Madras and at the Royapuram Hospital and I am also responsible for the lectures in leprosy to the medical students in the university. They have also roped me in as President of the Medical College Council Vellore and put me on the Executive of the C.M.A.I. (Christian Medical Association of India) so you will see that if anything I

42

have more work to do.

We long to get home as it is nearly six years since Cameron left us. I hope to send you some reports soon.

Our love to you both,

Yours ever,

signed Bob Cochrane"

By October 1943 a warm invitation came to Bob "to become the Medical Secretary for the Mission, at the same time being the Mission's representative at the Christian Medical College at Vellore, should that college desire your services."

Bob's reply from Chingleput was enthusiastic.

"I can hardly express the thrill your letter gave me, I always felt my true allegiance was with the Mission to Lepers. I regret my leprosy work has had no official connection with the Mission. My attachment to you personally made me more sorry this had to be. Now, when I was beginning to wonder if it is God's Will for me to go to Vellore, your airgraph comes with a definite proposal. I should like to indicate the trend of development in the Presidency. The time is coming, and perhaps more rapidly than we are aware, when it may not be possible to continue my research and widespread work for the Presidency and retain my position in this institution. It was this thought that largely influenced my mind in my acceptance of a post on the staff of the proposed Medical College. I am firmly convinced that my main work for a number of years to come will be in the Madras Presidency, for I consider that whatever the political developments, Madras Presidency will always be ahead of any other section of India. (This confirms what is said in the book by Jane Buckingham entitled "Leprosy in Colonial South India").

Further, leprosy has definitely got a place in Government thinking and in the medical curriculum. Such a place, that given time it should not be difficult to establish a complete system of leprosy control thoughout this Presidency, backed up by an educated public and medical opinion. I am also more than ever convinced that our duty as missionaries is twofold : 1. Widespread evangelism and 2. The setting up of definite pieces of work which will always act as a challenge and stimulus to the National Government, whose inescapable responsibility is the development of an adequate anti-leprosy organisation. Vellore offers me the scope and the independence and at the same time gives me the opportunity of retaining my position with the Madras Government so that a system which I am gradually developing will continue to develop under my direct guidance.

I wish to make my position very clear.

1. I should wish to be given a free hand to associate myself with any Government anti-leprosy scheme which they considered needed my attention in an advisory capacity.

2. In the development of the Leprosy Department of the Vellore Medical College I should look to the organisation of:

A) A leprosy hospital which would be an institution for special investigation and research and for dealing with specialised cases.

B) A rural leprosy unit which would be in connection with the general medical preventive unit – for I do not believe leprosy should be separated from general preventive medicine.

C) The establishment of a small home for derelict cases of leprosy which would act as an example to Government, indicating to them how this problem should be tackled.

Thus the Mission to Lepers would have on a Christian basis a unit which would cover every aspect and would, I feel sure, develop under God's guidance into a really first class demonstration of how the leprosy problem should be met. Under these conditions I should be willing to accept your offer, provided a mutual agreement could be reached with the authorities of the new Medical College at Vellore. In any case I should be willing to accept, on the above general principles, the Medical

Secretaryship of the Mission to Lepers even in the event of the Vellore scheme not coming to fruition. I am, however, under a deep sense of conviction that the latter is a very remote possibility.

It will be known shortly that I have been offered the position of Vice-Principal of the Medical College. As you know, if I have a work which is congenial, I have been given the inestimable gift of being able to put in longer hours than the average person, and therefore I do not anticipate any difficulty in fulfilling both posts.

Yours ever,

signed Robt G Cochrane.

A cable on 31st August confirmed his willingness.

"Gladly consider proposal available 1945 possibly earlier."

The reply was positive -

"At its October meeting the Council heartily approved of an invitation being made to you, and its general terms have now been worked out, and these I transmit to you for your consideration and acceptance or refusal.

Signed by the General Secretary.

A.D.Miller"

In June 1944 he made time to write a newsletter from Chingleput to friends back in England. He gave tribute to Dr. Ida Scudder, the founder of the Christian Medical College and Hospital and to her faithful companion, helper and supporter, Miss Gertrude Dodd, outstanding and courageous women.

Clearly there was a twinge of conscience as he started this long overdue letter writing;-

'My dear Friends,

I am afraid I have lost touch with many of you since the war began. Knowing that many of you are intensely interested in our work, I feel I must write and tell you as

45

briefly as I can, about what has been happening here in the last four years and acquaint you with our possible move to Vellore.

First with regard to the Lady Willingdon Leprosy Sanatorium. Thanks to the loyal and devoted staff I have been permitted to extend the work so that now, it can be said, that we have all the threads in our hands, and are ready as soon as the war is over, to place before Government an anti-leprosy Programme.'

Then as well as pointing out the Government's duty to secure and maintain a healthy nation, he looked at the financial side of the issue and said, 'If each of the Allied Nations were prepared to set aside one day's war expenditure for one week after the war, enough money would be found to deal with almost every medical and social problem! Prolong the war expenditure one week after cessation of hostilities and the money would be forthcoming!'

He ended with the conclusion that this may seem impossible to some, however, 'Unless we build up a first class personnel and functioning College, exhibiting the spirit of Christian Fellowship there will be far greater difficulties to face later. But if it has been achieved, then no national Government is likely to withdraw recognition, for its scientific contribution linked with its Christian service will be such that, seeing the prestige that a college of this sort will bring to India, will not lightly take a step which would liquidate it.'

The final page of the Circular letter mixed his great concerns for the work with some more personal and family matters.

'Another particular feature of the last two years is the number of service men who come into our house from time to time, some staying for a meal, some staying for up to a week or more. In addition to my ordinary work I am acting as Medical Officer to the R.A.F. Unit and this brings me in touch with the men fairly closely. Every now

46

and then we have airmen who are sick staying in our home, or in the home of one of our colleagues. From what we hear we know that several of them have been greatly touched by our simple little service in the Sanatorium and some have been led to a deeper spiritual life.

Please pray for us in all the work here and particularly in the new and very responsible duties, which we shall be embarking upon at Vellore.'

Then, lest it would appear that family were totally forgotten in the hectic lifestyle and heavy workload, mention of the children was made – Cameron as a senior at Christ's Hospital, Horsham, England; Ian now entered one of the senior houses at Scotch College, Melbourne, Australia ; 'and little Margaret in boarding school in the hills and had spent two months of this year in the school sanatorium with whooping cough. This long separation from our children is one of the hardest things to bear.

We cannot sufficiently express our gratitude to our friends in England and Australia who have been so kind to our children in our absence.
With affectionate greetings from us both,
Bob G Cochrane
Ivy G Cochrane.'

The estimate of two hundred visitors from the R.A.F.is not exaggerated, for the guest book of the time bore witness to the 240 or more, who did sign the book, as well as the ones who were not entered - if this visitors book is like most, with some forgotten until after their departure.

David, the cook must have been kept very busy and Ivy no doubt, did much to make the visitors feel at home. No doubt she followed them with her prayers, too, for sadly, she put a small red cross by the names of five of the visitors, indicating that they paid the great price in the war.

Entries in 1943 and up to October 1944 show that a constant stream of visitors came to Chingleput as well as service men, from other Mission hospitals in India and Burma, including Dr. G. B. Archer from Purulia, Bihar (as it was then) who stayed eleven days, sealing further the deep friendship and increasing shared knowledge about leprosy. Dr. Herbert Gass came from Chandkuri and was later to be a colleague at Vellore and Karigiri. Dr. Edward (Ted) Gault came from Vellore and was to be the first to live at the College compound when, by Christmas, the new bungalow was completed - a great friend of the Cochranes from then on. Joyce Sanders, the Pharmacist, also visited and cemented the friendship before they all worked together in Vellore. Undoubtedly they all went away refreshed, challenged and renewed for their various tasks, with fresh flowers in the bedroom for those who stayed overnight.

Even after the move to Vellore visitors continued to arrive as recorded from September 1944 onwards, with many service personnel amongst them. Medical personnel from Government, Missions and some dignitaries seemed to flock to the Vellore Hospital during that period.

In July 1943 the Journal of the Christian Medical Association of India, Burma and Ceylon contained an article written by Bob, his full medical degrees being appended to his name –MD (Glas) M.R.C.P. (Lond),D.T.M. and H(Eng), followed by his present positions namely:-

Chief Medical Officer Lady Willingdon Leprosy Sanatorium;
Physician-in-charge, Leprosy Department, General Hospital, Madras. Honorary Secretary, British Empire Leprosy Relief Association.

The article is entitled, "The Leprosy Campaign in Madras Presidency with special reference to Prevention".

He pointed out that although diagnosis and treatment were of interest to physicians, prevention was of great importance, especially in view of the fact that whilst advances had been made in treatment over the last 15-20 years, there still remained no sure remedy, and in any case only treatment will not bring the disease under control. He advocated 2 main methods for prevention;

1) The awareness of the public, by the use of slides for propaganda purposes but that too many before and after pictures might raise the expectations too high;

2) The training of medical personnel, both under and post- graduate.

He hoped that after the war it would be possible to extend the present 2 week course to 4 weeks for doctors at L.W.L.S. Chingleput. He closed with praise for the faithful workers, 'If anything has been accomplished in the last seven years, the credit is due to those who patiently and faithfully pursue the trying but important routine tasks, and give others the time to organise and develop the work so that we can all give our utmost contribution, and bring the day nearer when this fair land shall no longer be haunted by the fear of leprosy'.

CHAPTER 8

ADDED CHALLENGE

PAUL BRAND

Yet another very colourful strand was about to enter the story. His background was a very carefree upbringing in the hills of South India where his mother still lived and worked. Paul had grown up and gone to England where he trained as a carpenter, but then went for medical training at Leyton, in London. Then he specialised in orthopaedic surgery. His parents were devout Christians and he personally developed his own strong faith.

His book "Ten fingers for God" tells his story well.

"Then suddenly out of the blue came a telegram. 'There is an urgent need of a surgeon to teach at Vellore. Can you come immediately on a short contract? Signed Cochrane.'

But how did he happen to pick on me?" He would have understood better if he had heard a conversation which had taken place some months earlier between his mother and Bob.

"Would you be interested in having my son come to Vellore"?

"Certainly not, Cochrane had replied, "unless he has his FRCS."

"But" Mrs. Brand had shot back triumphantly, "My son has his FRCS." So enters Paul Brand and his wife Margaret to this fascinating story.

Presently Paul received a letter which said in substance, "I will meet you under the clock at Victoria Station at such and such time".

The two objections of military service and expecting a second child were both overruled.

The War Department bowed to the persuasion of a stronger will, whether of God (as Margaret devoutly believed) or of Bob Cochrane (as Paul secretly suspected) or of both which was more likely, since the two were presumably working in co-operation. (ibid, p66, 67)

So it was that Paul Brand travelled by sea to India.

It was perhaps a year after his first visit to Chingleput when Paul Brand decided that he was ready for the great experiment. "If you will send me a patient whose hands could not possibly be made worse," he said to Bob, "I'd like to see what can be done with them".

The amazing story of this young intelligent man can also be read in full in Paul's book.

In 1811 James Dalton, Surgeon in Madras, had identified the characteristics of leprosy - rough,scaly skin,numbness of hands and feet, offensive breath, frequently a hoarse voice, thickened ear lobes and large livid lumps all over the face, (page 8, Leprosy in Colonial South India by Jane Buckingham.)

In 1842 two Norwegian doctors gave a precise description in Bergen after studying patients there, as it was still endemic.

In the 1860s Dr Francis Day provided an account of British understanding of leprosy in Madras Presidency.

A report in 1864 by the Principal Inspector-General in Madras Medical Department was based on information from doctors caring for leprosy sufferers.

80 years later Bob arrived, then Paul Brand to take the work forward in incredible

ways.

In 1874 the bacterial cause was discovered by Dr. Armauer Hanson in Norway.
The term leprosy continued to be used in the 18th and 19th century for any skin disease with a repulsive appearance, affecting the whole body,and resistant to treatment. (ibid P9).

Understanding of leprosy increasingly gave way to a more scientific concept in the 19th century.

The Hindu Scriptures placed restrictions on leprosy sufferers right to inherit and even prescribed outcasting in some circumstances. (ibid P10).

ANOTHER THREAD

Ida Scudder, the daughter with a doctor father and grandfather, held her own with five older brothers. After training as a doctor, she felt a strong call from God to work in S India, where her parents worked. After five long years she obtained permission from the Surgeon General to set up a Womens Medical College. "You will be fortunate if you get 3 applicants, but if you get 6, then go ahead."

151 applied and 14 of the first batch graduated in Madras.
(Ida S Scudder of Vellore. P74.)

KEEPING HIS HEAD ABOVE WATER

Running the Institution at Chingleput was more than a full time occupation. Those working there, observed Bob's light on in the early mornings as he read the Bible and prayed and at night in the laboratory pouring over the microscope. This after work, giving time for tennis and sharing other recreational activities with staff and patients. The quest for a cure and progress with chaulmoogra oil injections urged on his endeavours. This daily work plus regular visits to centres at Saidapet, Kavanur and

Ranipet made his life extremely full. A sleep pattern of about 4 hours a night made this possible. Even in this Bob gives thanks to God for the blessing of "the inestimable gift of being able to work longer hours than average".

See Plate 11 Dapsone injections into lession.

Even before the move to Vellore had been finalised and negotiations were still going on, overtures were being made to obtain Bob's services for BELRA based back in England. If and when he left India they would be very happy to have his services, but with no intention of interfering with his present plans (TLMI archives - letter of 10.1.1943). Clearly his expertise and skills were being sought after from several quarters.

There was further correspondence concerning the termination of Bob's service with the Church of Scotland mission, and the desire expressed for everything to be done to the entire satisfaction of all concerned, with a smooth and amicable change over. The request came to take on the gigantic responsibility of being the Principal of the Christian Medical College Vellore, while its "Principal Emeritus" Dr. Ida Scudder was in America seeking additional support.

See Plate 13 photo of C.M.C. Hospital, Vellore.

To continue in the words of Dr. Pauline Jeffery in her book "Ida S. Scudder of Vellore",

'Meteor-like, Dr. Cochrane appearing in Vellore, assembled a staff to meet the demands of Government. In 1947 he flew to England for a two and a half month stay during which he interviewed the senior Directors of nine large business firms, wrote to about 100 firms who might be interested in leprosy work in Vellore and India, had numerous interviews with important statesmen, newspaper editors; Canon

Raven; Master of Christ College, Cambridge; the secretary of the Nuffield Trust; the Secretary of the Medical Research Corporation; and the Lord Mayor of Birmingham. In addition to all this he conferred with heads of eight large hospitals, and many other physicians.

All the interviews were held with the aim of interesting the folk of Britain in Vellore and developing research on the treatment of leprosy in India. He succeeded in persuading the various agencies interested in extending this research, so greatly needed in India, that Vellore was the logical centre for such a project because of the wide prevalence of this disease in the environs of Vellore, and also because of the effective work that had been carried on by Vellore since the early days. When he returned as Honorary Director of the Leprosy Campaign for the Madras Government, he asked to be released from being the Principal of Vellore Christian Medical College, but Vellore did not really lose him as the clinical work for his research for improving treatment of leprosy is now carried on in connection with the Vellore Medical college.' (ibid, p176-177).

The crisis that had drawn Bob to Vellore was created by a new law, signed by the Congress Leader, Dr. T. S. Rajan to abolish the Licentiate Medical Practitioner grade of medical education. No students were to be allowed to enter Vellore's portals unless the curriculum of the medical college was raised to the M. B. B. S. grade. Although this had always been the goal for Vellore, because of insufficient funds, it was as yet unattainable. But now with the stroke of a politician's pen, if Vellore was to continue, there must be a larger highly qualified staff, a larger and better equipped hospital, new pathological, physiological and bacteriological laboratories, and a research department. To offer more clinical material for the students the 268 beds of the hospital should be increased to 500. Even then only 70 of those 268 were endowed.

Already the existing plant was vital with inward growth. Every department clamouring for more space, more equipment, more staff. (ibid, p160)

Back in Vellore new tints were added to the spectrum. In 1944 Dr. Cochrane was persuaded to leave his post at the Leprosy Sanatorium in Chingleput to join the staff at Vellore in order to help in the gigantic task of making the transition from the L. M. P. course to the M. B. B. S., as well as to change it from a women's institution to a co-educational medical college, affiliated with the University of Madras.

In responding to Dr. Rajan's challenging legislation to eliminate L.M.P. courses in Madras Presidency, Dr. Cochrane and the Vellore staff girded themselves to tackle the difficult task - to train doctors and nurses to sally forth equipped with the Christian ideals of service and the best training possible to lighten India's burden of misery, resulting from superstition, disease, lack of hygiene, and lack of enlightened standards of living. (ibid, p170).

So we see that Bob left Chingleput to stay in Vellore not only as Principal of the college but also as Director of the Hospital. One could say that he was a glutton for punishment, or more accurately compelled to maintain his "hands on work" as well as the onerous duties in Vellore, as we see by the record of this era by Dr. Douglas Russell and Dr. Paul Brand who accompanied him on the trips not only to Chingleput, but to other places.

How indeed could Bob cope with all these great demands on time, energy and skills? It could be regarded as a juggling act, but I prefer to think of it as the power of the Holy Spirit infused in that daily walk with God in the early hours as he disciplined himself to manage with so little sleep.

As Isaiah says in the Bible, "They that wait on the Lord shall renew their strength." (Chapter 40 verse 31). Of course there were the cat naps in a chair after lunch for no more than ten minutes which appeared to refresh him. In India the chair of choice was a railway waiting room chair made of cane with a wooden frame and with two wooden planks for the outstretched legs, just right for men who like to sleep spreadeagled on their backs.

But back to Vellore, where tales abound of his daring driving to Madras at high speed to keep an appointment without allowing sufficient time for the journey.

Any journey in India can prove an unexpected adventure and the good spirits and humour that played such an important part in the arduous undertakings, hindrances and adversities, are shown in the following song which was reportedly sung by a team returning after a break down following a long days work,

'Keep on singing when the motor stops,
Keep on smiling when the back tyre pops,
Keep on hoping when the petrol drops,
And you'll get there
And you'll get there before morning.'

It is not difficult to see that in Bob and Dr. Ida there were great similarities of character and how they both saw the value of tennis as a recreation with their staff. Along with their great dedication and hard working ethics they were able to keep some time for play and socially mixing with their staff, in other words working hard and playing hard. (ibid, p175.)

"I never want to travel in the same boat as you" said Dr. Cochrane to 'Typhoon Mary' – an ex-member of the Vellore staff who had acquired a reputation for having survived a series of accidents, operations, diseases and broken bones, as well as typhoons and a close shave with a floating mine. "No," he continued with emphasis, "Never! You work your guardian angels over-time and all the guardian angels will be so busy taking care of you that they will have no time for me!" Typhoon Mary retired discreetly, but she knew quite well that if anyone tempted providence it was Bob.

VELLORE

Never let us despise the small early beginnings which under God's Hand can grow to something spectacular. In 1900 when Dr. Ida Scudder started a small dispensary in the corner room of an old mission bungalow, who could have predicted it would become a world famous hospital and associated Medical College?

The small town too, has grown enormously with all the growth of the hospital, and its need for supplies of all kinds. But 100 years before Dr. Ida appeared on the scene Vellore was a town with a reputation for a lot of "NO"s. As well as no hospital, it had a river with no water, a Hindu temple with no god (abandoned when the Moslem invaders had desecrated their exquisite stone-carved fort temple, by killing a cow in it, a hill with no tree, and a fort with no garrison. (Quote Dr. Ida Scudder of Vellore, India, p.164)

The upgrading of Christian Medical College Vellore to the university associated standard of M. B. B. S. and the change to a co-educational institution was indeed a tremendous task and this is a contribution from one of the first batch of male students through the portals of the previous all-female college.

PROFESSOR C. K. JOB

Professor Job wrote in 1986 as an obituary (International Journal of leprosy Vol 54 number 1 Page 116)

'My association with Dr. Cochrane dates back to May 1947, when he was the Principal of the Christian Medical College, Vellore, India. I belong to the first batch of eleven men students admitted to the college. He used to meet with us informally once every month under a mango tree on the campus. During that one hour of fellowship, he inspired us with his life's rich experiences and made us feel a part of the great institution. He refused to be addressed as "Sir", a term of respect, which was expected from a student, and insisted that we call him Dr. Cochrane.

He selflessly gave himself away in the service of leprosy patients. I often wondered how he could accomplish so much in so short a period. Then I realised that the secret of this strength and success was in his knowledge and wholehearted commitment to His Master, the Lord Jesus Christ. He firmly believed and demonstrated in his life that "All things are possible through Him that strengtheneth me". He was truly a medical missionary who placed his life in the hands of his Master and was used mightily in the service of leprosy patients.'

He further wrote in 2006, ending his tribute with this -
"Dr. Cochrane had many achievements to his credit, I would like to end by mentioning a few :-

1. Just like any great leader he invested in people to continue the fight against leprosy that he began, and succeeded in his crusade. He made leprosy an acceptable specialty to the experts in the medical profession.

2. He strengthened and established the Christian Medical College and Hospital on strong foundations when it was struggling in its early steps.   C. M. C. Vellore owes to Dr. Cochrane's dynamic leadership for its solid foundations laid again with trained medical experts inspired and recruited by him.

3. He built up the foundations of the Leprosy Research Institution at Chingleput so that now it is one of the most important leprosy research centres in India.

4. It is his vision which brought into being Schleffelin Leprosy Research Centre at Karigiri which is now one of the leading International Leprosy Research Institutions.

The history of leprosy and the fate of leprosy patients changed for the better because a person like Dr. R. G. Cochrane lived. God was glorified in his life.

C K Job. 21.6.2006."

PHARMACIST

Apart from Dr. Brand who with his F.R.C.S. was enticed to Vellore as a highly qualified surgeon, other unsung heroes joined the team. One of these was a well trained pharmacist, Irene Mills, known as 'Jimmy', who had the right qualifications in line with the Government of India's new policy for upgrading by having better trained staff. On arrival she was met at the railway station in Katpadi by Bob and as there was no other available accommodation she stayed with Bob and Ivy in the big bungalow at the college compound. Ivy was very kind and also insisted that she buy a topee, which she did. On seeing the topee, Paul Brand who had also recently arrived, filled it with plaster of Paris and then said, "Please take your coffee". The fact that she as a new, raw, young person was welcomed into the home of the Principal and his wife, and not only welcomed but made to feel completely at ease, made a big impression on her.

She had first met Bob in Brighton, England, when she had offered to the Methodist Missionary Society. The memory of that meeting was fixed in her mind as he went to buy bananas which were an unknown treat in those war days, and that they talked as they walked along rather than an intimidating interview type of meeting, which she would have found quite daunting. After she stayed with them, she stayed in Private Ward C, and there were rats everywhere!

She recalls having to deal with many difficult situations. One of these was having a senior colleague in the pharmacy with years of experience but not with the qualification of the "new girl". It was important as part of the upgrading of the hospital that there were qualified staff. The senior lady showed much Christian grace and the new girl had to exercise great diplomacy, as she learnt from her older colleague who was much more strict and on the ball. There were also staff problems with which she as the "In charge" had to deal with such as the discovery of misuse of drugs by a member of staff, requiring disciplinary action. Then another incidence of off–duty behaviour by one of the staff in the pharmacy, which was not in line with

Christian morals and behaviour!

Her next home was a shared bungalow with Miss Vera Pitman, who was the Nursing Sister in charge of the hospital. This must have been a great relief after the rat infested single ward room in the hospital itself.

Irene wrote, "Vera was an older more kindly person than you might expect as a Matron."

I can vouch for this as she much later in 1959 was a surrogate mother to me when our first son was eventually born by caesarian section in the early hours of the morning following 27 hours of labour. Vera stayed with me throughout the night and must have been very tired for the next day's duty. Maybe being Bob's daughter-in-law had something to do with it!

A sense of humour was also a great asset to those who worked in the field of leprosy. It helped them through very hard and difficult times but the spin off was felt by the patients they served. It was beneficial to them also, by treating them as fellow beings. Respect for their identity and worth, as co-workers in the scheme of things and definitely not underlings, helped to restore confidence and self worth. This skill was of especial value during the days of painful injections into lesions of the face, where the daily treatment verged on torture in the patient's mind, but was grimly endured in the hope of cure and being finally restored to family and society.

There is a misconception about leprosy being a disease of the poor. But we have seen that a university professor was affected by the disease, which caused a complete change in his life. This erroneous fact has added much needless misery to countless leprosy sufferers and their families over the years, causing needless ostracism and isolation.

It is always easy to be knowledgeable from hindsight and what we now know means that only 3 percent of the population are likely to contract the disease and the rest of us, whether we worked in the field of leprosy or not, are fortunate to be in the 97 percent, thanks to our wonderful immune systems.

We now meet another person who was unfortunate enough to be in the three percent, Dr. K. V. Desikan. Let him tell his own story.

ROBERT G. COCHRANE AS I KNEW HIM

"It was August 1947. I was then a medical student at Mysore. I was, all through, at the top of my class, and an object of jealousy to the competitors. The only little concern was a big anaesthetic patch on my left forearm. I did nothing about it because none of the doctors I consulted recognised the cause of it – not even my Professor of Medicine.

Such was the ignorance about leprosy in those days. Suddenly on the 15th of August, the day India became Independent, paralysis struck, affecting the muscles of my left hand. I ran to the Professor of Medicine and showed him. I do not think that even at that stage he could diagnose. He rushed me to the Superintendent of the hospital, Col. Nagendran, a surgeon. It was he who made the diagnosis, but did not disclose it to me. I was advised to go immediately to Vellore and meet one Dr. Cochrane who was a "Nerve Specialist". I believed them and thought that I am being referred to a great neurologist, for obviously, Col. Nagendran wanted the truth to be told to me only by the renowned expert.

I went to the famous Christian Medical College Hospital in Vellore. At the reception counter I asked for Dr. Cochrane's office. While I expected to be ushered into a posh consultation room, I was shown an isolated little structure far away in the corner of the compound. Such was the discrimination of leprosy patients even in a missionary institution! When I looked at the isolated building, my opinion about the stature of Dr. Cochrane came down. Anyway, I had to go wherever he was and whatever his specialty, of which I was completely ignorant. I met the receptionist and he asked me to sit on the bench. Wiping my sweat, I sat down wondering why I was sent to such a god-forsaken place. It was then that I realised for the first time what disease was suspected in me and what fate I was led into. I felt a reeling in my head. The ghastly picture of my future went through my mental eye. I would be thrown out of my college, being a leper. I would have to quit my home, and my dear ones and be cast in to a "leper home". I would develop hideous deformities as illustrated in the photographs. I did not have even the courage to cry. I sat dazed, prepared to hear what cruel judgement I would have to hear from the specialist.

Just then the real man entered the office. I was immediately called in and I stood before a big-built white man, Dr. Cochrane. He had a gruff voice. I was scared. He asked my name and other details. I was stripped and examined. Painful skin smears were obtained from different parts of my body and I was asked to wait, thereby increasing the suspense of hearing the final verdict.

After about half an hour when my skin smears were examined, I was called in again and asked to sit in a chair. Suddenly the gruff voice from the big man seemed to mellow. He sat on a chair by my side, and with his hand on my shoulder explained to me that I was suffering from an immunologically resistant Tuberculoid type of leprosy, that I am not an infectious case and that I could continue my medical education "without let or hindrance". With those words, he gave a written medical certificate. I had several questions to ask which he patiently answered. My fear of Dr. Cochrane slowly vanished and I realised that I was sitting beside a kind and generous man on whom I could fall back at any crisis in my life.

Back in Mysore I did not reveal my disease to anyone. Due to the prevailing ignorance, none of the college authorities suspected that I had leprosy. I somehow managed to complete my education and obtained a Medical Degree.

The rest of my life was a big saga as I entered into leprosy service. I had to face the implications in the society in the earlier years for being a known leprosy patient. However I rose higher and higher professionally, was happily married and occupied high positions in the Government, in the Indian Council of Medical Research, in the World Health Organisation and in International voluntary organisations. The work also brought me several accolades and the highest awards in leprosy. What a contrast it was from what I imagined on that fateful day. For the next 20 years after my first meeting, I met Dr. Cochrane several times at Vellore, Madras or at Chingleput. During those meetings I took the opportunity to learn about leprosy from him, by attending his clinics and his lectures to trainee doctors and medical students.

Once I asked him to arrange for me to work in China or Nigeria where there was a great need for leprosy doctors. His immediate response was, "Nonsense, you are not going to any other country. There is a lot of work to be done in India." That decided it, and I have so far worked for 55 years in India. He desired that I should work in the mission hospital in Dichpalli, in Andhra Pradesh, but I was committed to another organisation and preferred to continue.

Once at the beginning of my career, sometime in 1953 I had the privilege of Dr. Cochrane visiting my clinic at Sewagram. I showed him some of my patients and explained my work. He appreciated and gave some useful hints, I proudly placed before him my documentations and my careful recording of skin lesions neatly drawn with a green pen. He saw them and remarked, "The charting is good – if they are correct." I mentally felt like hitting him, but I was such a small fry before him and I should accept his remarks. Later while having lunch he advised, "Desikan, you must never say you are tired and sit down, but work till you are exhausted." I have followed that advice all through my life. In the evening when I was seeing him off he said, "You are doing a good work. If you continue to work diligently, I will present a camera to you." What a fine gesture!

In later years I met Dr. Cochrane in conferences.

My last meeting with Dr. Cochrane was in 1973 during the International Leprosy Congress at Bergen. At that time he was very old, age had taken its effect. He was no more his ebullient self. I was very happy to see him and went near him and greeted him with traditional Indian salutation. He recognised me and spoke a few words to me. Everyone came to meet him, and all knew that it was the last glimpse of him.

I never had the privilege to have him again at my clinic to find out whether I deserved to collect my camera from him, even though I met him several times at his clinic or at conferences. I admired him because he was one of those unique physicians who had the ability to combine a strictly scientific approach with the warmth of human feeling which was of utmost need with leprosy patients. He was one of the great founders of leprosy work in India, and set up a rich tradition for future generations of leprologists to follow. Apart from his own marvellous work in leprosy, I consider that one of Dr. Cochrane's greatest contributions was to stimulate several scientists, physicians and surgeons to take up leprosy work, and later make their own mark in the field of leprosy.

Dr. K. V. Desikan.

Chairman, Gandhi Memorial Leprosy Foundation, Wardha, Maharashtra, India."

So although he turned down the invitation to work in a mission leprosy hospital he continued to give many years of splendid service to the work established as a memorial to Gandhiji's wife, Kasturba, at Sewagram village in Wardha District. Again we can see that an apparent disaster in his personal brush with the disease was turned to great good so that this talented young medical student became a senior and well respected leader of the leprosy work in India, so dear to the heart of Gandhiji.

Purulia was the first place where Bob worked in India and had felt it had the potential for developing as a good centre for teaching. He regarded George Archer as an elder brother in every way, both personally, for the high standard of work and his fine Christian example. His sudden tragic death made him wonder about returning to work there after Vellore.

THE TWO PRONGED SEARCH

When Bob travelled in England to search for suitable staff for the Hospital and college in Vellore, South India, he contacted many people in different spheres to seek support and interest in Vellore, but also always at the back of his mind was the continued search for a more effective cure for leprosy. Part of his remit kept him in touch with drug companies. It was here that Imperial Chemical Iindustries came into the picture. Bob visited their laboratories in Wilmslow, Cheshire and was taken to see some cows who had been relieved of their mastitis by the parent drug dapsone. Bob was quick to see this might be a possibility to be used for leprosy. So when he returned to India he had a supply of it to use in trials. His quest to find willing guinea pigs was rewarded by the respect and esteem with which he was held by patients at Chingleput. Several of them agreed to try this new remedy. So began the use of Dapsone by injections in India, Africa and the U.S.A. The new drug was used under strict trial conditions, with the hope of it being successful. Reports were very encouraging, but after so many promising earlier attempts ending in failure, they were very cautious in making this exciting discovery made public too soon, for fear of yet another disappointment. Meanwhile the meticulous records would help to prove or disprove the efficacy of the latest drug, Dapsone. The question must have arisen many times in Bob's mind. Was Chaulmoogra oil treatment so promising to be now superseded by yet another triumph in treatment, using the sulphone drugs?

EUREKA

One guinea pig was a man who had worked in Burma, was now hoping to assemble a team to return to that re-opened country. However the unwelcome arrival of leprosy prevented it. He suffered much with the hundreds of frequent painful Dapsone injections and separation from his wife and young daughter, back in the UK. His cheerful face masking his sorrow. After seven long years he was reunited with them.

By 1957 a doctor doing out-patient clinics, then known as Roadside clinics in Vellore was to say, "You don't realise what a Godsend this new drug, D.D.S. is to us, showing the little white pills which have revolutionised the treatment of leprosy." ("Christ rides the Indian Road" by Dorothy Clarke Wilson)

A short time in England in 1945 was a time to be reunited with his oldest son Cameron, now a young man of 17 years old, after seven long years. It is impossible to imagine the trauma of such a long separation, for another father was shocked at seeing his child grown to a young person in his two years at sea during World War 2. It can only be hoped that it was not a repetition of what a young nurse whose parents were missionaries in China, was once heard to say, "My parents? I don't know them."

In this generation, unlike earlier ones, it is possible to ensure that in spite of physical and geographical separation, close links with the immediate blood family are maintained. No longer is sea mail known as snail mail, and not even airmail, now called snail mail, with the advent of electronic mail. We can only admire the complete dedication of those who have truly obeyed the call to preach the gospel to every nation, regardless of the great personal cost. The promise of Jesus recorded in St Mark's Gospel chapter 10 verse 29 says, "No man who has left father, mother, children for my sake and the Gospel's but he shall receive a hundedfold now in this time, brothers, sisters, children and lands, with persecutions; and in the world to come eternal life."

The truth of this promise has been proved by countless people over the centuries since it was said and written down for our benefit.

A letter of July 1945 mentions the possibility of flying back to England, and here again methods of transport are changing and making far-off countries more accessible. Hopes of getting to England before the visit to Vellore of the University Inspection Committee in October did not materialise, but later.

In the mean time there was another unexpected event which caused much pleasure. In a letter to the Mission to Lepers head office in London, Bob wrote,

"Thank you for your letter of 11.7.1945 and for your congratulations on my F.R.C.P. Do not ask me how I managed it, but it is not the result of an examination. Fellows are elected among the Members of the College.

I never expected to reach the distinction of being a Fellow of the Royal College of Physicians, but someone evidently thought I had been making quite a big enough nuisance of myself to warrant my name going up for election to the Fellowship. I know no more about it, but naturally while I do not feel I deserve this honour, I am very pleased.

All the best,

Yours ever, Robt. G. Cochrane."

(TLMI archives ref 35/63.)

CHAPTER 9

THE DREAM HOSPITAL

As if juggling all the five different jobs he was handling was not enough, Bob persisted in looking for a hospital where the dreams of a research and Treatment Centre specially for leprosy was established and recognised for its own worth and value in the total scheme of Medical work and practice. This was yet another dream, which was fulfilled and doubtless inspired by the development of the college and hospital in Vellore and support of those who also favour this development.

TYPICAL LEPROSY HOSPITAL LOCATIONS

Traditionally when Government or private land was obtained for the use of leprosy patients it was always at a discreet distance from towns, markets, and public places to avoid the uproar of the public opposition of such a place being built near *their* domain, and Karigiri was no exception. Several sites were suggested and viewed with the eye of future development by the leprosy experts in Vellore. Various agencies had to be approached for funding and as usual, the larger the committee the more difficult to obtain a united concensus of opinion, let alone a unanimous one. Here again the hand of God provided the unity of purpose and the acquisition of a site for building.

Finally Karigiri was the site chosen, being several miles from the hospital in Vellore town and also some miles from the Medical College. Karigiri was a small village which had a well established pottery, famous locally for its ceramic magic water pot. The village was mostly surrounded by paddy fields, which were irrigated by a channel feeding water pulled up by two bullocks from a large well.

See Plate 15 photo of Robert with Dr H Gass and Mrs Z Gass at Karigiri.

Inevitably the site was a barren, remote area not easily accessible except by the dirt track from the main road where the bus stop was situated. Trucks rumbled along the track raising clouds of dust and delivering the required building materials. Apart from the supervisors of the building, the experts in Vellore awaited this further development with great anticipation as they continued to work in cramped limited facilities at the hospital compound. Gradually the building took shape until the hospital was opened.

There are always teething problems with new buildings, new projects and developments, and Karigiri was no exception.

Many of the patients came to the hospital with severe foot ulcers due to the lack of feeling. The long walk down that dusty track from the bus stop (if they had been fortunate enough to be allowed on to the bus with smelly ulcers covered with dirty rags) only aggravated their ulcers and prolonged the stay in hospital.

So a bullock cart was then used as a local bus/ taxi service to transport patients to the hospital and then return them to the bus after outpatient treatment. This greatly helped to prevent the ulcers becoming worse rather than better on their trips to hospital.

A staff bus carried workers from Vellore in the morning and returned them in the evening after a day's work. Gradually staff quarters were built and some staff relocated to Karigiri, travelling into Vellore when working there. So there was much coming and going as the staff adapted to another change in their lives. The long straight road became a busy thoroughfare raising many clouds of dust as vehicles, as well as the patients' transport, delivered medical supplies and sacks of rice to feed the in-patients. A staff canteen also provided a welcome coffee break.

Patients admitted for reconstructive surgery as well as care of ulcers kept the staff busy and while they were all beavering away downstairs there was much activity upstairs. Here there were animal houses with mice and an armadillo for research. One day a clack–clack sound was heard on the stairs. The armadillo had escaped from its quarters. Fortunately the many mice did not repeat the escape act or there may well have been female screams!

So the dream came true for a Research and Training Institute where many people from different countries and with expertise in various disciplines (doctors, nurses, therapists, laboratory technicians), came to benefit from this new establishment known as the Schieffelin Leprosy Research and Training Sanatorium (S L R S). It is named after Dr. William Jay Schieffelin who was a founder member of the American Committee and then President of the American Board.

The excellence of the work and training were recognised by the Government of India and indeed only after completing the 6 week course on Leprosy for Medical Officers, could the hospitals where they worked claim the per capita grant made from the Government. The small village and its postman could not cope with the amount of mail generated by letters from many different countries around the world, so the large hospital now had its own Post Office!

Bob, meanwhile, had inspired, enthused and trained suitable staff to build up and maintain the standard of excellent practice to make it worthy of the only Government recognised Training Centre in India. It drew trainees from much further afield, but the recognition by the Indian Government was also an encouragement for other Governments to use it and so, due to the status awarded it by the Indian Government, it attained international recognition.

During this period of great activity and progress Bob somehow found time to write various articles. One was in April 1943, which appeared in the Indian Medical Gazette, entitled 'Some Aspects of Tuberculosis Infection in Saidapet, following a survey between July 1940 and March 1942.' Saidapet is a suburb of Madras (now Chennai) and it is interesting to note the occupations listed. Top of the list comes dhobi (washerman), second is public scavenging on city rubbish heaps. In third place there was weaving and last the milk trade. (This was long before the Western Health and Safety standards were introduced.) This really shows the type of area and the marked poverty of the people living there, eking out a living at subsistence level, so no wonder there was tuberculosis. It is also interesting that the credit for the article goes to the Medical Officer at the clinic with Bob added as Officer in charge, under the Indian Research Fund Association.

The Christian Medical Association of India, Burma and Ceylon Journal contains an article by Bob in January 1945, concerning "Vellore: an urgent situation."

It provided a map of the hospital and another of the College campus and a short plea for United Efforts Now.

He called on all members of the C.M.A.I. for their support for this huge financial outlay. The cost was expected to be five lakhs (one lakh being 100,000 rupees) of which three lakhs were in hand. He ended the article, 'in all our efforts to create here a hospital of outstanding merit and a college of privileged uniqueness, let us not fall in to the temptation of worship at the altar of scientific efficiency and medical perfection. Satan will try and make us forget that God dwells in the heart of the humble, and blesses him who is of a contrite spirit. Our greatest danger lies here, for in our zeal to make this place successful, we can so easily put in to the background of our mind, that we are called by God to this high endeavour, and forgetting, forfeit God's leading and guiding. Only with Him in all our planning, thinking and living, can we succeed.'

As World War II continued to rage, the battle against leprosy was also accelerating. The latest new drug, Dapsone, was now being used with encouraging results. Dr.

Stanley Browne was involved in a trial in Africa, and Dapsone was also being used in other countries, including America.

Bob's expertise and knowledge of leprosy in many of the countries where it was prevalent contributed to the International Leprosy Congresses held regularly. In 1948 it was held in Cuba where many Leprologists gathered to share their knowledge and experience with the latest developments shared and new possibilities explored. Dr. Colin McDougall was working in Zambia and much correspondence flowed between the two men. He felt that the three great facets of Bob's character were,

1. His ability and authoritative way of engaging with people in high places, whatever their expertise and wherever in the world they were.

2. Getting leprosy in to mainstream medical practice, rather than it being Cinderella.

3. His desire to 'marry' the scientific approach and the philanthropic approach.

THE MOVE TO VELLORE

This had clearly been an important step and it is signified by a new page in the Visitors Book with Ivy's clear caligraphy in large, bold print: AUGUST 1946.

The first entry being Laurie Baker from Fyzabad, U.P. - Mission to Lepers. He as an architect had designed many of the mission buildings, there and in Allahabad, also other places such as Champa. M.P. The plans for extension and new wards in Vellore would have kept him very busy, and then later the buildings at Karigiri.

Many people were drawn to visit, some on official business for the hospital and patients; others as friends and associates. Dr. Catherine Young travelled all the way from Chandag Heights, Pitlogarh in the Northern Hills. It is not clear whether she was coming for hospital experience or for her own personal medical needs, but she stayed for eight days, before making the long return journey, which probably took a week.

During her visit Rev. H. V. Shepherd also spent a couple of days in their home, giving as his address "Ex Burma" rather than Chingleput.

One of the early visitors was Dr. V. R. Khanalkar from Tata Memorial Hospital Bombay - a specialist in cancer who became very interested in leprosy and contributed a huge amount.

In February 1947 is the bold, clear signature of Ian H. Cochrane and he gave his address as Scotch College, Melbourne, Australia. where hand writing was given much attention and its importance stressed, so as a result his hand writing is very clear, unlike his Father and most other doctors.

Bob was clearly excited at the prospect of seeing Ian again. Many people knew that he was coming from school in Australia, so when Paul Brand arrived on the scene, people all thought he was the eagerly anticipated son - a mistake he went along with by calling Bob 'Dad'.

Dr. Katherine Young made her long journey from the Northern hills and Dr. Victor Rambo and his wife Louise from what was then called Central Provinces. The hospital where he worked gained some renown for its eye work, and he for his vital living faith and relying on the power of prayer. Once when travelling to a remote clinic in the jungle, the vehicle broke down with no hope of getting it repaired, his travelling companion recalled, who was an able mechanic, until Victor said, 'Let's pray', got down on his knees and prayed with the authority of Jesus for the vehicle to get them to the people in need of their help. Within minutes, the problem was solved and they were on their way again rejoicing. A lesson in faith and prayer that his companion never forgot.

Other interesting entries include Gypsy dancers at College Hill, Rev. and Mrs. Ison, from Sydney, but working in Faridpur, E. Bengal (now Bangladesh).

Havana, Cuba was the venue for the International Leprosy Congress in April 1948, where Bob gave an address on the Comparison of Sulphone and Hydnacarpus Oil therapy of leprosy.

The only mention, for the purpose of this book would be that, he gave the results of years of work and the results of treatment to show that the Indian racial group responds better to hydnacarpus therapy than Europeans, and generally poor results in the Anglo-Indian (Eurasian) group. He gave acknowledgements to many people who helped to produce these results. July 1948 was when Chingleput was again the address for visitors, this time no caligraphy, but the name in Bob's familiar scrawl and date, for Ivy and Margaret moved back to England and he escorted them as far as the ship in Bombay (now Mumbai).

1949 brought visitors from centres in India to attend a Mission to Lepers Regional conference, and doubtless many others not recorded, without Ivy's watchful eye to do the honours.

On January 26th he wrote to thank the Mission for the Christmas gift of a book "Albert Schweitzer, The Man and His Mind".

He looked forward to reading the book, 'with great interest and I have no doubt, considerable profit'. (TLMI Archives Jan 1949)

Early that year Bob expressed his concern about certain developments in Government circles and the under-staffing of some of the Mission centres, stressing that work of the mission centres must be of a high standard, as an example of how the medical work should be done.

A month later he again wrote of the turmoil of his present situation and that a decision was still awaited from Central Government concerning the establishment of

74

the Central Research Institute at Chingleput.

A week later he received a letter acknowledging a copy of his article on the two and a half years experimental work on the sulphone group of drugs, with the original sent for publication in the journal "Leprosy Review", and also a copy of the missing letter. A letter in March 1949 from Mr. Donald Miller showed the great respect with which he regarded Bob in agreeing to withhold printing an article until they had met to discuss it, after sending Bob a draft copy. Their united desire to serve the best interests of the mission and leprosy sufferers is very apparent, as they sought to co-ordinate their efforts.

In April 1949 the long awaited document from the Medical Secretary was finally received by the Mission to Lepers in London.

It was entitled "WIDENING HORIZONS", and was an attempt at an appraisal of the present position of the medical work of the mission with suggestions as to future policy.

This 18 page document took some time to prepare and must have taken a similar period for the head office in London to read, mark and digest. All its contents were full of details concerning the present state of many of the mission homes he had already visited, comments and his recommendations for their future development, or curtailment. He regretted that his work at Vellore and Chingleput had prevented widespread visits. However the details he gave indicated that he *did* visit many of the homes in certain areas of India.

The political situation called for sensitivity and discernment, for it appeared to him that there was a concerted effort by the Government to take things under their control. This was not surprising in view of the recently declared Independence, 15th August 1947, being the official celebration. He stressed the need to stay closely in touch with the Government and to ensure that institutions were run efficiently and well, as an example of how leprosy work should be done, and not warrant displeasure by inferior work or unseemly behaviour by 'guest workers' in the country. The Government was seen to be embracing the responsibility for the leprosy programmes. It was encouraging to see National and International Organisations being established, like Akkil Bharat Kushti Samiti (All India Leprosy Society) and the Hind Khusta Nivaran Sangh (Indian Leprosy Relief Association) and a move to dissolve BELRA (British Empire Leprosy Relief Association).

Both were emphasising the need for relief, rehabilitation and after-care, while Government should be responsible for the more technical aspects of the leprosy campaign, and Government to ensure adequate medical standards in leprosy homes (Resolution passed at the All India Leprosy Workers conference in Calcutta). Unless the mission homes could make the grade they might well be closed down or handed over. "Today in India, it is, more than ever, the life that counts. We, as missionaries, I believe, are called on not to meet need, for need can never be met, but to demonstrate how leprosy work in all its aspects should be done. And in the words of Mildred Cable 'gossip the Gospel'."

Education of the public concerning leprosy should be increased with suitable literature.

See Plate 8 photo of Robert taking photo of child patient.

TREATMENT and RESEARCH

Basic research re-started after the Manila conference in 1931 and was largely stimulated by the International Leprosy Association.

His enthusiasm and hopes led him to declare, 'Today we are on the edge of advances as great and as productive as those of the early pioneers of the 19th century.'

Plate 1 - Thomas, Edgar and Robert

Plate 2 - Robert, Edgar and Thomas at Hither Green

Plate 3 - Thomas and Robert as teenagers

Plate 4 - Robert as a medical student

Plate 5 - Robert as a doctor (by Messrs Elliot and Fry Ltd)

Plate 6 - Robert on mule in N. Indian hills

Plate 7 - Robert with nurse Emilie Lillelund at Vadathorasalur

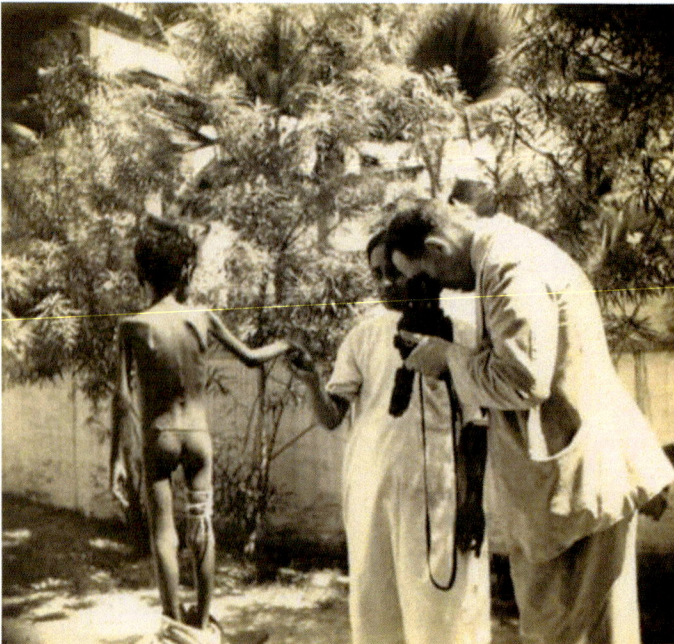

Plate 8 - Robert taking photo of child patient

Plate 9 - Robert examining child patient in Vadathorasalur

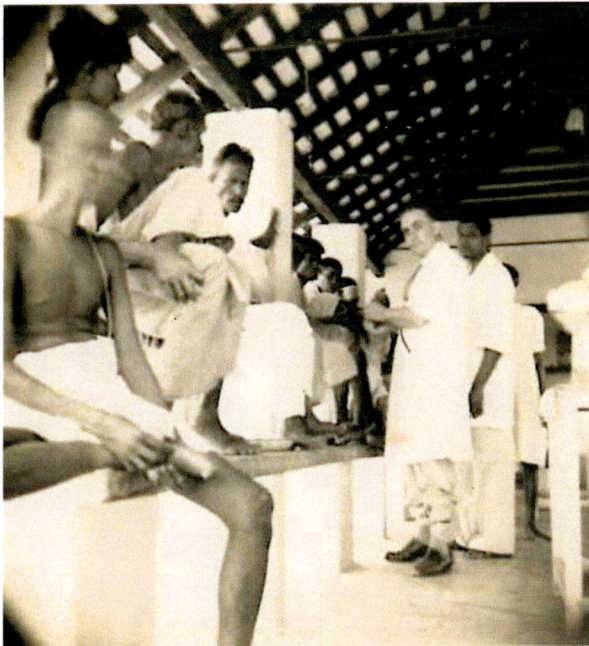

Plate 10 - Robert doing ulcer round at Chingleput

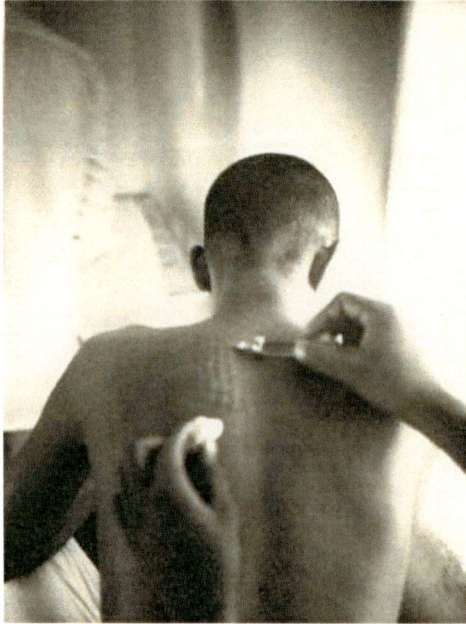

Plate 11 - Dapsone injections into lession

Plate 12 - Dr Ramanujam co-worker who called him "guru"

Plate 13 - C.M.C. Hospital, Vellore (courtesy of Wellcombe Library)

Plate 14 - Robert with the much used MacArthur microscope

Plate 15- Robert with Dr H Gass and Mrs Z Gass at Karigiri

Plate 16- Robert with Damien Dutton Award in Carville

Plate 17 - Robert with Stanley Stein, first recipient of the Damien Dutton award

Plate 18 - Robert examining African patient

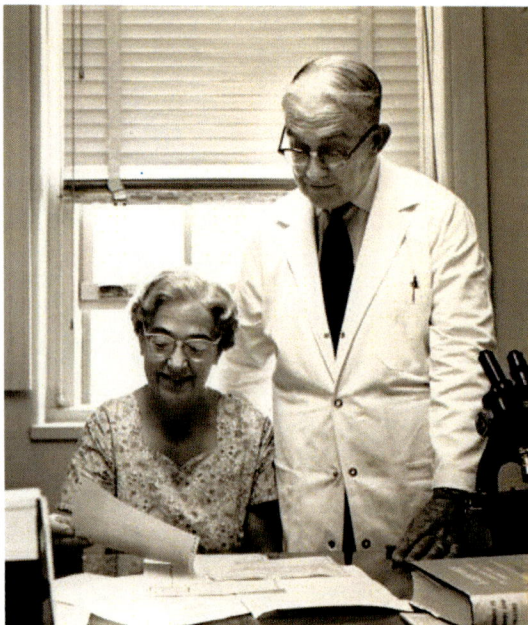

Plate 19 - Ivy sitting reading reports at "The Rooms"

Plate 20 - Robert dictating to Eileen Ball at "The Rooms"

Plate 21 - Robert in typical pose after examining patient

Plate 22 - Dr E.P. Fritschi consulting Robert in Vadathorasalur

Plate 23 - Robert addressing I.L.C. London 1968.

Plate 24 - Opening the Robert Cochrane annexe, Slade Hospital, Oxford 11.8.70

The new drugs were so effective that it was hoped to set up clinics in remote areas and he felt could even have the opportunity to enter lands closed to foreigners.

'Recently I was in Almora and Dr. Kate Young, the intrepid doctor of the frontier between India, Nepal and Tibet, came to meet me. It was a privilege to discuss many things with her.' He was encouraged that these border inhabitants, being of the Mongolian race, responded better to the new drugs, which was just as well, there being so many of them. 'When I return I propose to help Dr. Young set up a treatment centre on the very borders of Nepal itself. Let us pray that the results will be such that rumours of the work being done will reach Kathmandu itself. I leave to your imagination to picture the untold possibilities and the possible results of this in relation to the Kingdom of God.'

See Plate 6 photo of Robert on mule in N. Indian hills.

ADMINISTRATION

When only care was given and no specific treatment was available, supervision of the Homes was regarded as a part time and not full time occupation. So there were Honorary Superintendents who visited regularly but did not live on the compound. This was rapidly becoming unsuitable, for changes and developments require constant supervision.

On the other hand, ineffective work, due to shortage of staff or any other reason would be the opposite of the widening horizons envisaged.

TREATMENT

Medically he saw the need of a completely new re-orientation of the Mission's position in view of the great advances made in knowledge of the disease and its treatment. He appealed for consolidation of the total work.

Reports on visits to individual Homes fill the next few pages of the report.

Vadathorasalur Child Leprosy Centre was deemed an excellent choice, should the Karigiri option not materialise, for several reasons. It was situated in a highly endemic area, it had plans for suitable hospital and laboratory facilities and had the most experienced nursing sister, the Danish nurse, Miss Emilie Lillelund.

See Plate 7 photo of Robert with nurse Emilie Lillelund at Vadathorasalur.
See Plate 9 photo of Robert examining child patient in Vadathorasalur.

Poladpur in Bombay Presidency was considered too isolated to develop being 'too far off the beaten track. As a most loyal servant of the mission Dr. Victor Das' services are not used to the best advantage.'

His dedication was matched by his wife, Beulah, who journeyed there by bullock cart after their marriage, and the packing boxes were then used to make furniture for their primitive home. Learning Marathi and the isolation were a test of faith for this young married couple.

The journey up north to the United Provinces meant long journeys and many changes of transport to reach the northern hills. Dr. Kate Young travelled to meet Bob in Almora, where they had good discussions. There is no mention of riding a mule on this trip, as he did for the hospital opening in Chandag, the following year, with amusing consequences.

TRAINING

This was a priority in Bob's mind for the future of the work, where Mission workers needed to be fully equipped, trained and updated in the most recent treatment and trends, to take the work forward. He made several suggestions for suitable places, one being Purulia, Bihar (now W Bengal), stressing his strong belief that one place should be selected so the training was consistent for all the staff from various centres. This training centre should be in addition to the proposed Government one at Chingleput.

The report concluded, 'The horizons for the Mission to Lepers are widening, but to take advantage of the new situation, bold planning, far-sighted thinking and a set determination that our policy must be to emphasise the approach of the Gospel of Christ in every aspect of leprosy work without reduction of medical efficiency. May God himself guide us so that through His Holy Spirit, an era of still greater service will be heralded and we shall not find that our work will gradually be replaced by Government institutions and we have to ultimately abandon the great field of India, the birthplace of the mission's activities.'

Spiritually also he felt there was a challenge to face changes.

During the summer of 1949 Bob made a trip to England and apart from some time with the family he found it quite difficult. For one thing he was away from his much loved India and the all-absorbing task there, and for another, he had no office base and secretary on whom he relied very much. However, as Medical Secretary he was able to use the mission head office and avail himself of the secretary to the General Secretary of the mission with whom he was on such good terms and considered a close friend, as well as a colleague with such similar views.

The paper he prepared for the Mission to Lepers in September contained detailed instructions for using the various derivatives of sulphetrone and ended with a word of warning about the possibility of reaction to these drugs, and the precautions required. (TLMI Archives Sept 1949).

This paper was delivered at the Annual Meeting of the mission held in May.

By October that year Bob was back at Chingleput and received a letter from London concerning amendments to a new edition of "Leprosy and its Challenge" which were felt to be too lengthy to include, however the photo of the author showing the proper method of giving an injection was to be included. A proof copy was to be sent by air-mail for Bob to have the final say. The fact that Bob lay a strong emphasis on the spiritual side of the work, particularly at the end was appreciated. Bob wrote to London concerning the finances both personal and for the building of the research Unit at Karigiri. He was not optimistic that the amount allocated for the purpose would be sufficient for an effective one, but fully realised the limitations of the mission in this respect.

The question of who should be the builder was also discussed and one suggestion was that Mr. Jagadisan might be contacted as he built the Kasturba Gandhi Home for women and children, reasonably and satisfactorily.

The type of buildings for staff and patients, were suitable for Indian staff and could be adapted for European staff. (TLMI archives Oct 1949.)

He also clarified that the supply of Sulphetrone granules was to be supplied by Burroughs Wellcome, indicating that the company would keep this stock always available, so that he could obtain it when required. He would need to know the sum of money available for the purpose before starting the most important infectious patients on the treatment. (TLMI Archives Oct 1949)

1950 saw Ivy keeping the home fires burning in Bromley, and a continual stream of visitors at Chingleput.

QUO VADIS- Where to ?

Now that the College in Vellore had been upgraded and staff assembled to do the teaching and provide the practical teaching on the wards for the needed subjects, The

Leprosy Hospital for treatment, research and training established, Bob felt his task had been completed. For he came with the intention of staying for a limited time only, to meet the challenge of the crisis. He was ready to step aside and hand over to others to continue what he had instituted with God's help and the support of many praying friends.

RETURN TO CHINGLEPUT

Shedding the heavy responsibilities at Vellore, a return to the 'hands on' work he loved at Chingleput could have meant a slightly easier lifestyle and workload in 1948, but that was not Bob.

His family were in England and he was able to give more time to the hospital patients, whom he also regarded as friends, but also the extensive and time consuming research work, peering down his microscope for signs of leprosy germs, noting their numbers. Always interested to note the progress of his patients, and encourage their improvement with the results the microscope confirmed. Social life was confined to the hour of tennis, which gave him some much needed exercise and much pleasure to the other tennis players, staff and patients alike. His renown was spreading far and wide as indicated by the number of addresses given and papers written for medical journals and other publications. Behind the scenes we have to remember the faithful army of supporters and long suffering typists who worked equally hard to keep up with copies of addresses and updating patients' records. We must also remember the faithful prayer warriors who prayed for him and his family as they shared in the efforts and progress being made, not forgetting Ivy who was such a great woman of faith and prayer. Only God could have empowered the determination and strength, which enabled these gigantic tasks to not only be attempted, but accomplished. Bob daily claimed the sufficiency of God for the task as he waited on Him in the early hours. His humble faith was richly rewarded.

Along with his duties at Chingleput, he continued as the Director of the Madras

Leprosy Campaign, his lectures at Vellore and Madras to students - except when time ran out and he had to phone Dr. Douglas Russell to stand in for him at Vellore. It appears that the telephone system worked quite well, as yet another aid to his multi-tasked work. His visits to clinics and Units continued also. The gad-fly continued to work in many places, by stimulating, challenging and inspiring.

Bob's typed letters to Donald's substitute, Mr. Hayward in January 1950 mentioned financial matters and also a possible physiotherapist.

He was also quick to commend his courage in being willing to take on these huge responsibilities.

The following month Bob wrote that he would much appreciate a physiotherapist to do the research work he considered essential. However he considered a 70 year old dentist too old for any work on the mission stations. So it is interesting to note that Dr. Ernest Muir went to Purulia at that age and was able to work in the hospital by day and in the evenings play chess with the Nursing Sister!

He again expressed his great appreciation for the efficient way the work had been handled during the General Secretary's absence.

In April 1950 a letter from Donald Miller contained a rather wistful comment, 'I suppose that as I write you are nearing the end of your journey across the hills, back to Almora after the opening of the Mary Reed Memorial Hospital. I shall look forward to hearing from Dr. Young. I am sure that your visit to that out-post station will have both been an inspiration to you and a real encouragement to those who live there. It is a wonderful journey, isn't it, and I do hope that you found Dr. Young in good condition.

I can fully understand your concern to be with your wife and children at this stage of their development. I trust that you will feel all along that you are working within the Will of God, and that you are right in feeling that God is calling you out to some wider sphere of service in the next few years, as you put it. It is good that you plan to keep me in touch with developments.'

By October 1950 Bob was back in Chingleput after his visit to England. He had been busy with the third All India Leprosy Workers Conference in Madras, which Dr. Muir attended. They were able to discuss their plans for the following year. Dr. Muir planned to leave Purulia on March 8th, and since Bob was not anxious to overlap, he suggested the first two weeks of February be spent getting everything straight in Chingleput, then visiting a couple of Mission Homes on his way north to Purulia by mid March. He also expressed his great desire to be back in England by May 1st for his second son's 21st birthday. He hoped to find resources to fly about 24th April, since it was too late to obtain a sea passage. He would only expect the mission to pay the equivalent of the sea passage.

"All these arrangements are, of course, dependent on when the Ministry of Health desire my services." (TLMI Archives)

So it was now apparent that he was to be appointed to the Ministry of Health in England.

By the end of the year there appeared to be a problem with the Indian Government's Order to withhold grants to institutions if certain criteria were not met. Bob felt a strong line must be taken for he was convinced it was the Government's responsibility to finance the leprosy programme.

He suggested the mission withdraw from some of their centres. Yet he knew that the Government would be unable to provide sufficient staff and facilities to carry on all the centres. Bob was anxious to put the record straight and apologised for the misunderstanding caused by his private communication to the Surgeon General in Madras. He had been requested to do this, but it put him as well as the Surgeon General in a difficult position, with the Government Order already given. Fortunately diplomacy and openness won the day.

JANUARY 1951

Betty Marcroft typed a letter to Dr. Paul Brand from Chingleput concerning a proposed grant from the Indian Medical Research Council which had been recommended at the meeting in Agra in November 1950.

Bob pointed out that he had relinquished some of his salary from the Mission in view of an increased Honorarium from the Government in September 1949 and that Vellore had agreed to set aside this amount for leprosy work. He was now suggesting that this amount be used as a contribution for building a house for a member of the Leprosy Enquiry Team and to pay a salary to a laboratory technician for one year, at the rate of Rs.130.00 a month, so using the exact amount of money.

His understanding was that the technician would continue the work he had done for four years.

He mentioned Dr. Herbert Gass as the present lecturer in Leprosy and Dermatology at Vellore. He also was now keenly interested and involved in the research into any changes in the skin cells in relation to the type of leprosy. He would be the clinical advisor to the Leprosy Enquiry.

Bob hoped that this would enable the valuable research to continue. (TLMI Archives) By the end of January 1951 there was a letter from the General Secretary of the Mission concerning a passage home for Bob on the "Circassis" in March with a fare of £90. Mention was also made of the passage money sent earlier for Mrs. Cochrane and Margaret in 1948 and for Ian in 1949 from India to Britain, in 1949. Bob had financed Ian's travel from Australia to India, when he left Scotch College in Melbourne.

The General Secretary ended his letters with all his good wishes for the last two months in India, and reading between the lines he realised there would be mixed emotions, having had the same experience.

CEYLON

But by mid February Bob was writing to tell him that through the World Health Organisation, the Ceylon Government had confirmed their invitation to advise them on their leprosy campaign. (TLMI Archives)

It meant that he had to regretfully submit his resignation as Medical Secretary to the Mission,

The reply to his letter of resignation was sent to Colombo, in his new position as Director of Medical and Sanitary Services, with a copy to Mrs. Cochrane in England. It accepted, but regretted that it was due to his new appointment and the fact that as Medical Secretary of the BELRA he needed to reside in England.

The Council of the Mission recorded their gratitude and appreciation of his services. There was also to be a short article in the magazine of the that time produced by the mission called "Without the Camp".

Just before leaving his beloved India to return to England, via Ceylon for two months, he received the award which he most treasured. It was the Kaiser- I-Hind Medal in Gold – First Class. This was awarded for his outstanding public services. So from the days of 1928 when he obtained his M.D. on his thesis about leprosy following four years of work and study, his drive and professional standing had played its part in developing an upgraded Medical College, establishing a Government Research Centre and the possibility of fulfilling his dream to find a cure for leprosy.

However, the quest for greater knowledge about the disease by research, widespread acceptance of leprosy into the mainstream of medicine and the removal of stigma remained. Much work was still required to monitor and maintain progress. The challenge of leprosy remained.

So ends the chapter of service in India and also with the 'hands on' experience with patients in the Sanatorium.

CHAPTER 10

LONDON BASE

The eventful years in India, the country of Bob's adoption, came to an end and the parting was not easy, but he knew it was time to move on when the Vellore College and Hospital had been re-organised to meet Government standards; the Research and Treatment Centre established in Karigiri and the Leprosy Sanatorium at Chingleput was to be a Government–run Research Centre. Teams of well qualified staff were in place.

After all, one of his maxims was, "To show how need can be met, not to met all the need." In this next chapter of his life he certainly did provide general principles to serve as a rule or guide, as his travels took him even further afield during his next appointments.

The persistent desire for continued research into this fascinating disease with so many unanswered questions remained paramount. Yet another important need was increasingly impressed on him - that of teaching medical personnel the latest knowledge about the disease and its treatment.

True to form he continued to have more than one task at a time. A family base was in Bromley near London. This enabled travel into central London either by train or by car. His lifestyle did not lend itself to regular train times as he continued to work very long hours, packing in, to quote Margaret Brand, "Two weeks' work in one".
The train was suitable for son Cameron, now a medical student at St. Bartholomews Hospital in central London.

Not for Bob, who never mastered an Indian language, for the simple reason that no tutor was willing to come at 4.30am to give a lesson, this being the only time he could offer. A reliable car and a long-suffering, prayerfully supportive wife, helped him to continue his late nights and early mornings of work, travelling not only to London, but to visit patients around the country as well as the established hospitals for leprosy in Redhill and East Hanningfield, near Chelmsford in Essex. But at least they were now in the same country and most nights he was able to return home. There were nights when a sofa sufficed and made an even earlier start possible from London to the north or wherever the patient lived. Often visits were dovetailed with other appointments, some with doctors, others with pharmaceutical firms. One thing is certain is that there were no wasted moments, and there were always the 'cat naps' to refresh him for the next task.

B.E.L.R.A. AGAIN

"The next three years he resumed his contact with the British Empire Leprosy Relief Association as its Medical Secretary. But he had other irons in the fire. He founded the Leprosy Research Fund in 1951."

So wrote Irene Allen, the hard working lady in the office of the organisation now known as LEPRA (Leprosy Relief Association).

After his death there was established a fund in his memory, called the "Bob Cochrane Fund for Leprosy". This is administered by the Royal Society of Tropical Medicine and Hygiene, London. It provides up to three annual scholarships for leprosy workers who need to obtain practical training in field-work or research and/or experienced leprologists to provide practical training in a developing country, up to £1,000 each – a facility worth exploring for a thesis on the medical aspects of Bob's life, leading to even more modern advances in treatment and research.

She continues, "Based in London Bob was being called upon increasingly by Governments and Missions to advise on their leprosy programmes and to conduct seminars.

He was a most stimulating - not to say, provocative lecturer. He kept himself up-to-date and encouraged clinicians and others to interest themselves in the disease that he himself found so fascinating. It was he who first pioneered the use of Dapsone in India, still standard therapy for leprosy.

He also saw the possibilities of what was then known as B663 and persuaded Dr. Stanley Browne to conduct clinical trials in Nigeria.

It is now known as Lepromin (or Clofazamine). This drug is generally recognised as an excellent anti-leprosy drug with anti-inflammatory activity. This development made inexpensive outpatient treatment possible for many people with leprosy."

THE ROOMS

His work in London, from 1951 was based in Wimpole Street, parallel with Harley Street, where a valuable and equally hard working lady acted as secretary, by the name of Eileen Ball.

See Plate 20 photo of Robert dictating to Eileen Ball at "The Rooms".

Her duties were many and varied, the actual typing of letters, reports and documents for publication were just a small part of her admirable work. She acted as chauffeur to and from the airport, so Bob could give instructions and dictate letters into his little dictaphone up to the last minute, when he would hand it over to her for typing during his absence.

She went far beyond the call of duty as visitor to patients when Bob was unable to do so. She was a receptionist for anxious patients arriving to have a consultation; telephonist, assistant and so much more. In these days she would perhaps be called an office administrator, but no title quite sums up the contribution she made to "The Rooms" as they were known, and to the total impact of Bob's work.

In the words of her brother, "Eileen was Secretary, Chauffeur, Receptionist/Hostess, and friend to Bob Cochrane and worked for him for just over 10 years during the 1960s – 1970s. She would often work long hours from 9.30am to 7.30pm or even later. During this time Bob was employed as a Leprosy Consultant by the N.H.S., looking after the leprosy patients in England and any new ones that might be diagnosed. One of Eileen's tasks was to care for these patients. There was one in particular, by the name of Dolly, whom she used to take out to meet other people - thus spreading the good news that leprosy was not contagious. Eileen also took every opportunity to spread the word that leprosy could be cured, at the same time emphasising that the word 'leper' should never be used.

Bob was fortunate in that he could take a 15 minute 'cat nap' during his travels and wake up as fresh as a daisy.

Sadly Eileen was not endued with the same physical stamina as Bob and after this strenuous time suffered two heart attacks and had to leave for a quieter, more local life where she lived.

In addition there was a laboratory assistant to deal with the many sections sent by post, or taken by Bob, to be stained and checked under the microscope for reporting. Bob would then dictate the findings and Eileen would type the letter which would be mailed or air-mailed to the person concerned with the good or bad news of the results. So, true to form, Bob relied on team-work to get the job done and help him in his arduous task, which was anything but routine.

See Plate 19 photo of Ivy sitting reading reports at "The Rooms".

It would appear that the document he prepared concerning among other things the need for a leprosy officer in the UK, was in effect, his job description. He was appointed as an advisor to the Ministry of Health on leprosy. He did visit as a Consultant; patients were referred to him by General Practitioners and others around the country. He saw patients at his consulting rooms in Wimpole Street and welcomed doctors and other medical workers to learn something of the disease prior to their service overseas or to update their knowledge before returning to duties overseas. This in addition to the processing of material sent from leprosy centres around the world, kept Bob and his team of staff very busy.

LIVERPOOL CONSULTATION

Here we find another strand of colour added by a young nurse studying tropical medicine and working in a Liverpool hospital. She writes, "The course was a very practical one and sailors were admitted from the ships when they came into port from various countries around the world. A variety of tropical diseases were treated. I was on night duty when a very ill European who had been teaching in Indonesia arrived. This man had been treated for a long time, for a number of diseases of the skin before the correct diagnosis of Hansens Disease (leprosy) had been made. He was a very ill man, in reaction (from the leprosy germs at war with the drugs within his body). In those days, even in the U.K., leprosy was a disease with a stigma and he was isolated in a small room. I remember it well for I was isolated with him, to care for him. Dr. Bob came frequently to advise and to monitor his progress, and I saw first-hand that he was an expert in his field, who cared enormously not only for his patient's physical health, but also for the whole of his need.

Two years later, in 1961, at a Leprosy Mission Centre in South India, called Karigiri, my husband and I had the privilege of getting to know him as a colleague and friend. He was also 'Uncle Bob' to our children. His manner sometimes appeared to be abrupt, on first meeting him, but in reality was a very gentle and kind man. Indeed he was a great man, and servant of Our Lord Jesus." So wrote Mrs Elsie Harris, the widow of Dr. John Harris, who also worked tirelessly for leprosy until his sudden death in Africa.

LEPROSY RESEARCH FUND

We have already seen the great emphasis Bob laid on the need for research and to this end he used any personal money he could to further his collection of material, such as slides for viewing under the microscope, photographs, records and x-rays, all carefully catalogued and stored for future reference. So the amount of material in his collection continued to grow.

See Plate 14 photo of Robert with the much used MacArthur microscope.

One of the visitors at Chingleput in November 1950 was a Dr. W.A.R.Thomson from London and Nottingham.

So when the Leprosy Research Fund was established Dr. Thomson became the Chairman of the Committee. First steps towards establishing this were taken in 1953. It was made possible when Bob was appointed to the staff of the American Leprosy Missions Inc., as its Technical Medical Advisor. In that capacity he was able to continue his studies and relate leprosy to general medicine. It could prove of value to leprosy workers, leprosy organisations and also show that leprosy touches many aspects of medicine, rather than merely a tropical disease of little consequence. An additional benefit to drug manufacturers would be that with the preliminary work done they could launch their full scale investigations more promptly, so saving them time and money.

The financial contribution from American Leprosy Missions Inc. and from the Wellcome Foundation enabled Bob to establish more suitable accommodation for a Laboratory and Consulting Rooms at Weymouth Street not far from the current rooms in Wimpole Street.

The aim of the fund was to establish small pilot projects of research for a short period. If such projects showed good results and signs of requiring further study and development, they could seek funding elsewhere as a going concern, already proved to be worthwhile. Others less productive could be dropped, without further investment of time and money.

Similarly, trials with new drugs could be undertaken and developed further if found suitable. In other trials there could be a comparison of the effectiveness of the new drug compared to the Sulphone treatment currently in use.

The seeds of interest and bringing in other medical specialists were beginning to bear fruit, for again Dr. V. R. Khanolkar came into the picture. His visit to Chingleput earlier established a vital link between the two men. Here was a man dedicated to the pathology of cancer and doing a great work in Bombay as the Director of the Indian Cancer Centre. Somehow Bob enthused him with the desire to also get involved in leprosy as well. In 1954 he visited London and Oxford, had discussions with Bob and others and drew another person into the picture. So it was that Dr. Graham Weddell from Oxford was also drawn in to the pursuit of research in leprosy. He visited India for 3 weeks. His quest was to find out if leprosy could be used as a tool in his research about the nerves of the skin. So it was not only the interest of another scientific worker aroused but his findings as a result of that 3 weeks investigation proved facts about the sensation of leprosy patients, which was often badly affected. Another person was drawn in to research through Dr. Weddell's work, Dr. Jamison. A Research Fellowship enabled him to travel to Africa where he spent three months collecting material from Nigeria. It was hoped this would trigger a better understanding of the way the disease develops from the first moment it enters the skin.

Gradually the team of researchers was increasing and the picture of leprosy in different countries was emerging.

The latest addition to the growing team was Dr. E. M. Brieger. His visit to Belgian

Congo from Cambridge in 1955 was a direct result of the Leprosy Research Fund. It also provided an exciting possibility of using an electron microscope to study the life history of the leprosy germ, for he found a well-equipped hospital with highly motivated staff there. This in turn led to a further grant for two years from the Colonial Medical Research Council.

The worldwide web continued to thrive and grow, as a year later another doctor travelled to South Africa. There, thanks to the co-operation of staff at Westfort in Pretoria, he was able to collect material to do a study, in detail, about an injection called lepromin. The injection of tuberculin is used to test a person's ability to resist tuberculosis or show a possible infection due to a severe response to the injection.

In the same way, lepromin could give an indication of the person's resistance to, or infection with leprosy. This doctor made two visits to Africa and also attended a conference on Leprosy and Tuberculosis, whilst there. So yet another expert was sufficiently challenged and interested to get involved in leprosy research. You could say they became 'hooked' as so many have been once embarking on the study of this elusive disease. Bob was keen to get results from Dr. Kuper, both to determine a person's ability to resist the disease and also as an aid to 'classification'. The experts were able to put the various signs and symptoms of the disease into groups. The number and size of patches, the areas of the body affected, the state of the nerves and skin all had to be included in the examination as well as what the microscope revealed about cells in the skin. All these gave a clear picture of the patient's progress. Later it would also be the means of deciding which course of treatment they should take.

Rather like a difficult jigsaw puzzle each piece was important to fit in properly and to build up a picture of this rogue disease. The patient work of Bob's for years, peering down his microscope and recording the results were the foundation on which all these doctors built their increasing knowledge. Yet another outstanding expert was drawn in by attending a conference about the body's response to the Tuberculin injection. So the problems of the two diseases were being better understood. Later Dr. Hanks visited the Johns Hopkins Leprosy Research Unit in Jhalda, West Bengal, India.

Bob was also aiming to set up a registry of all the mass of material, rather like a reference library, which would be a great visual teaching aid to new workers. It would also build up a picture of the variations of leprosy in different parts of the world, of which there were many. Bob's aim for this Fund was that leprosy would be regarded on an equal footing with other tropical diseases such as malaria and tuberculosis.

(TLMI Archives)

MORE TURMOIL

Bob found leaving India traumatic and as all those who have worked overseas usually find, adjustment to life back in the old home country proves difficult. He had little time to brood over the situation but in the midst of all his activities he found time to write to the General Secretary of the Mission to Lepers. Now that he had officially left the organisation, he still retained his interest in its aims and work. Moving on to the wider horizons that he felt right at this stage in his life and the development of leprosy work, there were some hurt feelings.

Somehow he felt that all his hard work over the years in India were not appreciated. This was due to the fact that it appeared his suggestions for policies and progress in the work of the mission in India were not being followed.

This was mainly in the area of drugs used for treatment which was, after all part of his 'dream'. This dream appeared to him to be shattered. He mentioned much earlier that he and Dr. Muir did not see eye to eye on some matters. So after Bob left India there was naturally a type of vacuum in medical leadership. This appears to have 'rocked the boat'. The situation was aggravated, in that a document Bob promised on one of the drugs never seems to have been written or arrived. This left the mission in a predicament as the non-medical leaders sought to carry on the work without Bob's strong guiding influence, in the many homes around India. It appears that the advice of Dr. Muir, the older leprologist was adhered to, not surprisingly, in the event, and this upset Bob considerably. He felt disappointed that his efforts had been wasted, as his many suggestions have not been taken up. The policies and principles by which he had worked appear to be ignored. As such a dynamic and controversial medical opinion it is surprising that there is so little recorded about these disagreements, which must have occurred from time to time.

But again we see the integrity of the man who was not able to keep this to himself, but wrote quite openly to the General Secretary, his old friend and colleague.

The letter must have been difficult to write, and was typed by Ivy for it came from the Bromley address appropriately named "TIRUMANI" as in Chingleput, S. India.

It was doubtless written after much thought and prayer. He mentions the drug in question – Avlosulphone and points out that he is not against its use. His letter continues with the fact that it is only going to cost, perhaps, marginally more – an extra Rupee a year per patient - than the sulphatrone injection. He is always conscious of the costs involved as well as seeking the best possible solution for the patients. He writes, "I feel it would not be honest, or in the interests of our friendship, not to give you some idea of my sense of disappointment. But I assure you whatever I say, in this letter does not affect in the least bit our personal relations, and I shall always have the greatest affection and regard for you and the work which you are so sincerely doing." He also writes, "I do not wish to be a pessimist, but I think we may find that Homes will repeat our experience that D.D.S. is not always the ideal drug. They may find, in many cases, they will have to change to sulphetrone or some other compound. It would surely have been wise to indicate to the Homes that valuable as DDS is, it is not necessarily the ideal drug under all conditions.

With all good wishes, Yours very sincerely

Bob Cochrane"

(TLMI Archives)

Personal relationships are regarded as top priority and the letter of July 23rd received a reply written on the 25th July by the General Secretary.

These were the days when personal secretaries typed and returned the dictated letter for signing and posting the same day. One such person worked in the office with three successive leaders and maintained good relationships throughout her long and dedicated service. Even in her retirement Miss Pyle worked on the archives which have proved such a great source of help here.

The prompt reply included the suggestion of liasing with Dr. Herbert Gass still working in Vellore and keenly interested in the work of Karigiri also.

TIRUMANI. BROMLEY. ENGLAND

Visitors continued to be a part of the Cochrane family life, but not in such droves as in India, which was probably just as well for the domestic help was absent and the family was now five or rather six, for the dog Titch had joined the family. Bob continued to travel around England but touched base quite frequently. A few of the visitors came from overseas, and naturally most of those were from India or those who had worked there and were now, like Bob back in the U.K.

Those who were taking a well-earned rest from their arduous duties in the heat of the plains, found rest, refreshment, good company and ample food there. Many times parents travelled long distances to visit or collect their children from the boarding schools, situated in the cooler Nilgiris (Blue hills) of south India. They also were welcomed.

Staff of Vellore Christian Hospital and other Leprosy Hospitals in India, found a warm welcome at Tirumani and who would all have enjoyed a renewing of friendship so firmly established.

Mr. Fred Carswell and his wife Ida gave three addresses! One was the Jordan Hospital, Redhill, their native town and one was Naini, Allahabad, UP India.

Another visitor was Dr. Ida B. Scudder. She was the niece of the founder of the Christian Medical College Hospital, Vellore. Her valuable contribution was in the field of Radiology. At this time X-rays were used more, since this was before the days of cat scans and other more modern methods of investigations.

A HAVEN OF PEACE

Bob's regular visits to the Homes of St. Giles must have been an encouragement to him and also to the staff and residents there.

An atmosphere of tranquility pervaded the whole campus, as the Sisters went about their daily care of the patients, sustained by their faith and devotion.

The bell calling them to the chapel for prayers and devotions was heard regularly throughout the day from the early morning till the last prayer at night. After the furtive existence of their lives before admission there, it must have helped them to regain a sense of worth and dignity. One of the people who had been living in constant fear of his disease being discovered was Peter. His life had started well enough with a good education and then a well paid job in India, where he decided to stay after his father returned to England. Life was good and he enjoyed it until the signs of leprosy appeared. Then it became a nightmare. He moved from one set of rooms to another hoping to hide his illness. Eventually when money ran out and life became intolerable, he cabled his father to ask for money for a passage back to England.

The voyage back was mostly spent in his cabin - how different to when he set out on his career with great hopes and expectations. On arrival he was whisked away and ended the journey by night in a taxi. Like the worthy gentlemen who went in search of a secluded place to buy this property, the taxi driver also got lost. When he stopped to ask the way, his passenger, relieved it was dark and hiding behind dark glasses heard the reply, 'Oh you want the leper place', and duly gave directions to St. Giles.

Peter recalled, 'I think at that moment my life reached a depth of misery and degradation that it had never known before.'

The doctor had said to him, 'don't expect miracles my boy, but this new treatment really gets results.' He was referring to the DDS now in use.

(Archives of Sisters of the Community of Sacred Passion in a book called The second Miracle.)

The new life that Peter experienced is a book well worth reading if you are fortunate enough to find it or any of his other books such as 'The Seventh Gate', 'The painted leopard' and 'Young man in the sun'

The Homes of St. Giles not only brought him peace of mind, and a measure of healing, but also helped him to discover his talent as an author. His name appears in both Bob's and Ivy's prayer diary.

On a visit to the Sisters living in retirement in Sussex, their lively interest in the patients was still very evident. They could recall things that the patients had said such as, 'There is more life in a packet of seeds than in me.' So said Mr. Price. However they added that he took up marquetry, so it could well be that he was the

99

one who made the beautiful inlaid coffee table presented to Bob. So in spite of his low self-esteem he must have had some latent talent which was brought out at St Giles.

ADVISOR TO THE MINISTRY OF HEALTH.

In this capacity Bob kept up a flow of articles on leprosy for publication in medical journals, attended meetings in London and Geneva, made consultancy visits to leprosy patients around the country and always made time for his microscope. It is small wonder he saw little of the family and yet he loved them all dearly.

FURTHER AVENUES FOR RESEARCH.

Medical scientists were coming on board in London and Oxford as enthusiasm grew. Bob found it a thrilling saga and his zeal and enthusiasm acted like a magnet to other enquiring minds.

By 1953 he had yielded to the overtures from American Leprosy Missions Inc. to become their Technical Medical Advisor. Their interest and financial help enabled him to develop the Leprosy Research Fund into what became known as the Leprosy Study Centre. Here, with increased facilities and better premises the work expanded rapidly. Courses were held for doctors, nurses, technicians and others. A huge library of slides was assembled and the laboratory work was ably handled by Dr. Douglas Harman. He had worked on Hay Ling Chou, the island in Hong Kong where a leprosy mission centre was established.

The Cochranes attracted many visitors to their home and place of work, and that trend continued with many spending time at the Leprosy Study Centre. As biopsies continued to arrive from the four corners of the world, the mass of teaching material increased, not to mention the workload. In one year twenty doctors from fourteen countries sent 514 specimens to the Centre. These all had to be examined, reported on and then the results posted off along with a set of slides for teaching purposes.

Many names are recorded of those who learnt about the disease, how to prepare the slides for viewing under the microscope, treatment regimes and many other important matters.

When asked for her memory Grace Bennett wrote, "I went to his rooms, taken by Dr. Stanley Browne, I remember Dr. Cochrane being ready to share his knowledge and experience to help me in the situations we faced in Korea. I remember he was a gracious man of prayer and he wore 'spats'.

It is not clear whether he felt this appropriate dress for his position or for warmth. Most likely the latter as he felt the cold very much.

Dr. Gerald Wilson also went there for instruction before he left for further training in India and service in Taegu, Korea. His ten years service with the Mission to Lepers, with his wife Shirley made a big contribution to the work in Taegu. His memory was of the teaching to himself and Ian Cochrane, followed by prayer for the two men setting out on their careers in leprosy. Humility and dependence of God were very evident in Bob's life. Others were taken to the Jordan Hospital in Redhill and to St Giles for 'hands-on' experience. More than 40 research workers also visited, in connection with their particular area of interest ranging from drug trials to pathology. It was not all serious work though, for Bob always had a great sense of humour and a fund of amusing stories and anecdotes to share. Many seemed to concern food and misquotes of familiar sayings, such as 'you have buttered your bread, now you must sit on it.' And the boy who did not speak the King's English being corrected, 'don't say but - ER, say BUT-TER, after which the boy dutifully repeated, BUTTER is that bet- ER'.

During this time in England he also found time to write four articles for the paper "Life of Faith". About The church's contribution to the ministry of healing.

These appeared in print in September and October 1953 (kindly supplied by Agnes Alcorn from her late husband Bob's meticulous filing system.)

Also at this time a revised version of the booklet for circulation "Leprosy - Its challenge and Hope" appeared at the Mission to Lepers in their office in London.

He wrote, 'It is fascinating to trace the challenge of Christ, as represented by his servants, in this matter of leprosy, from St. Francis of Assisi to Father Damien and Mary Reed: and the story is not finished. I wonder if it is realised that many workers in leprosy have been Christians who have had a definite call. Of the seven well-known British Leprologists, five have been Christian missionaries, three serving under the Church of Scotland mission for many years. The Doyen of leprosy research, Sir Leonard Rogers, is himself a convinced Christian.'

He continued (in 1953) to write 'there are at present between 120 and 200 cases of leprosy in England and Wales; but all fresh cases which have been discovered, have up to now contracted the disease abroad.' He went on to describe the present knowledge of the disease and its treatment. He quoted others who had done outstanding work, such as Dr. John Lowe in West Africa experimenting as far back as 1948 with D.D.S. He also mentioned the treatment given at Vellore and Chingleput in 1946. He mentioned the dangers of high doses of the drugs and the need of preventive measures. There was a photo of boys receiving their medical discharge certificates from Purulia as the disease has been arrested. He stated, as he did in the articles of the Life of Faith paper that we should remember that disease, tragedy, disaster are all signs of a world in chaos, produced by man's rebellion from God. He continued, 'In my long years of leprosy work I knew that many of the patients at Chingleput wouldn't recover and some would inevitably die a horrible, choking death.' Yet he saw in the lives of those who trusted God the face of Christ in their suffering.

He ended with the challenge, 'Let us pray that by the help of Almighty God we shall continue to seize these opportunities for fresh service. So that in these changing days we shall bring to the poorest and most needy, not only the best medical care and the benefits of research, but also the riches of Christ Jesus Our Lord'.

CHAPTER 11

AFRICA TOUR FOR AMERICAN LEPROSY MISSIONS INC.

DAR-ES-SALAAM

Arriving at Dar-Es-Salaam by ship with his wife Ivy and daughter Margaret, cabin luggage was quickly cleared through customs, but not 2 cases from the baggage room. The next day these were also cleared and Bob was pleased that no bags were opened as empty plastic containers to send specimens to Dr. Weddell in Oxford might not be understood.

On arrival at the hotel there was a cot in the bedroom, hardly suitable for a trained nurse! A replacement bed served for one night for Margaret before moving to the Government House for the week-end. Here the family, and even Bob relaxed on the beach and some swam. On the arrival day Bob had wasted no time in meeting a doctor to plan the tour and visiting the Automobile Association about the Chevrolet Station Wagon due to arrive by ship in a week's time.

A phone call from a local doctor, whose wife had trained at CMC Vellore, invited him to a British Medical Association dinner. Here he met the Mayor of Dar es Salaam, the Governor of Tanganyika (now Tanzania)) and a young lawyer.

After the meal the Governor gave an interesting and amusing speech followed by the band from Government House. When the band started to play the March of the VIth Battalion of the King's African Rifles, of which he was the honorary Colonel, he took the baton and conducted himself. In bed by 11pm, which was early for Bob, he felt he was a reformed character!

The next 5 days were filled with meetings and business concerning the tour and the vehicle. An experienced driver/mechanic was engaged. Further trips to release the vehicle were required as the engine number was not on the invoice. Finally it went for some adjustments for the safari and the family went shopping. While the ladies bought supplies for the journey, Bob enjoyed visits to Indian shops and they also enjoyed talking about India.

They attended a Bible study where they met Government servants, Indians and missionaries, demonstrating the unity in the Protestant Evangelical Church.

SAFARI

The safari started with 120 miles, once the 22 pieces of luggage were loaded. They stopped to admire the beauty of Chazi and see the institution with its nearly completed hospital, the gravity-fed water system being of special interest. Bob regretted that the annual Government fee for water could have been better spent on improvements to patients' quarters or medicine.

Seeing patients always renewed his desire for hands on work. He also felt there was great potential for development of a teaching programme being near Dar es Salaam, if a doctor and nursing sister were provided.

The trend was set for early starts, long drives on poor roads and visits to other centres in Tanganyika (now Tanzania). They included Dodoma, Iambi, Tintigula, Singida, Tabora and Sekonge. In each place patients were examined, advice and encouragement given to staff and patients, recommendations made for unified efforts and precious samples obtained for research.

See Plate 18 photo of Robert examining African patient.

BOB'S CONCERNS

Helpful advice on treatment was only the start. The fact that healthy children were living with patients needed to change. Better segregation of men and women patients was needed to prevent many illegitimate babies.

OFFICIAL PLANNING MEETING WITH DISTRICT COMMISSIONER

The meeting in Singida was delayed until all the committee members arrived but future development plans and training were discussed. Bob strongly recommended a central leprosarium where resources could be pooled and training given. The 5 missions plus BELRA could make a strong team.

After the meetings a strong recommendation was sent to American Leprosy Missions Inc. for financial support to the proposed new centre at Iamba. It is interesting to note that even in 2009 such efforts were still being made in other areas of the world. Sekonge got a special mention for its neat, tidy village type houses for about 400 patients. Of the many institutions visited around the world Bob felt this Moravian Mission came top. The Nursing Sister was asked to send pictures to show in USA and UK.

BORDER FORMALITIES

Official Papers were needed before leaving Tanzania, a Pass for Bob from the District Commissioner and papers to allow re-entry for the driver. This brief interlude enabled the family to meet a Government offical – a fellow passenger from the ship, who was also a keen Christian.

Shopping included a new glass for Bob's watch, broken when removing a fallen tree from the road.

LEAVING TANZANIA

The saga of early starts, muddy roads (with the monsoon), broken bridges and diversions, all conspired to delay the journey. The District Officer greeted them at the Government Headquarters in Kibondo, formalities were completed and they headed for the border to enter Burundi. Each border had two posts,one for leaving the country, and after no mans land another border to enter the new country. Thankfully they finally arrived to unpack in Nyankanda, only to find an Asian flu epidemic! This gave the tired travellers time to rest, and for Bob to attack the huge mail pile. "A blessing in disguise," Bob said.

Dr. Allan Bapty arrived with his wife but returned to his hospital due to the flu epidemic. His wife remained and later, gave birth to her daughter.

Bob's next journey was to the Protestant Alliance conference where his address focused on unity. He spoke about the importance of small things, like the rudder turning a huge ship. He was ill at ease about the topic, not knowing their problems, but relying on all his experience and God's guidance from the Bible. His message was well received.

In conversations he found similar problems to earlier days in India and China, where the need for less foreign domination and more local leadership was expressed.

Bob felt the only way to overcome shortages of staff and supplies was unity. In his father's words, "We need to plan strategically in terms of the total church." A difficult talk given fearfully, not only well received but with his feeling such freedom of Spirit in the doing. Time to work on the manuscript for his book followed. The minifone reels were constantly being posted back and forth to London for him to check and busy secretaries to type.

Returning to Nyankanda work revved up. Margaret had worked hard on preparations for surgery, both patients and the theatre cleaning. Two nerve operations were done one morning and in the afternoon there were visits to patients' families by the river. Morality was high and seldom were there illegitimate children. Bob was greatly impressed by the simple faith of those who met in the evening for fellowship, and their willingness to talk of their faith, truly planted. Here is the strong power and influence of the native African Church .

Allan, able to speak Kirundi, helped much in the operating theatre and in the preparation of the Teaching Course. Bob found his eagerness to learn prevented any restiveness when checking cases.

TRAINING COURSE

He found this strenuous, but wanted to make their week away from work and arduous travel worthwhile. He was happier with the practical applications than the theory and academic side of introductory lectures. Practical demonstrations also took place.

Patients who received their discharge certificates left to return to their villages, and some took their new found faith with them to face a difficult home coming, due to the continued stigma of the disease.

There was a pleasant little interlude with a third birthday celebration for a staff child. If you don't believe God is in total charge and plans every detail of our lives as his children then read this.

'His most prized present was a tractor. Little did we realise we had bought the very thing he wanted'.

The American style cake was 'guaranteed to put on pounds !!'

A QUIET SUNDAY THEN FURTHER CLINIC VISITS !

Early Communion, a morning service and preparing a talk for the evening, meant no time for reading and writing.

Examining patients for discharge Bob was sad to note a high deformity rate only topped by Japan and Korea.

At a staff meeting Bob urged seperation of healthy and infected contacts, with a possible 'well village' and a 'rehabilitation village'.

Margaret was able to re-organise ulcer care and staff training for it, in Nyankanda.

BOB'S CONTINUED TRAVEL TO NIGERIA VIA CONGO

After a long, early drive to the border at Usumbura, office, bank and other offical work had to be done before the onward flight to Leopoldville and connecting flight to Kano, Nigeria. Here the sad discovery was made - no squashy bag, which contained all the precious teaching materials, diary and other irreplaceable items. The long suffering host received a rather disconsolate Bob at almost 2 am! At least he had the minifone reels so could continue to correct the manuscript. Two days later Bob and bag were reunited, with great relief.

TRAVEL BY BOAC

Better on a camel, being Bob's name for it!
One delay of 24 hrs gave him another day at hospital work, but another meant 12 hours at the airport, with little hope of connecting flight to Robertsville, Liberia.

LIBERIA VIA GHANA

In Accra, Ghana, he stayed in a hotel to await the next flight. He was relieved that air conditioning was not too cold! Although he would have preferred to be in a Guest House or private home, he conceded that after 2 very short nights the Lord was giving him a rest. On arrival in Robertsville airport, he shared a taxi into Monrovia, as no one met him. He stayed in the same place as 2 doctors going to Ganta for the Leprosy Training Course, a remote place with no regular mail service apart from willing travellers.

The Teaching Course was appreciated by highly intelligent assistants, but assembling patients for the demonstrations had been a bit problematic at the start.

Back in Accra, Ghana, he shared a hotel room with another doctor, for a short night.

After posting samples to London next morning, Bob went at high speed to another well organised institution run by a small staff, a tribute to what one person can achieve.

Back at the airport that evening he and other waiting passengers were relieved when the DC7 finally landed safely in spite of an electrical fault with the undercarriage, as it had circled many times. This and remedying the fault delayed departure.

CONGO

The delay meant arriving in Leopoldville at 3am. Here the patient man from the Baptist Mission, Mr. Moore, was waiting for Bob and his two companions. After only an hour in bed, Bob was awakened by the sound of heavy rain. The weary Mr. Moore took him back to the airport for the connecting flight to Usumbura. Reaching the airport was very difficult for there was 9 inches of rain on parts of the road. On arrival the usual entrance was quite impassable, so they were directed to the back of the airport. Here, after removing his shoes and socks, Bob was helped with his luggage by the kindly Mr. Moore to get into the booking area of the building. There was a three hour wait, due to flooding of the runway. The flight itself was a rather bumpy one, so many passengers were travel sick, but not Bob. Landing soon after 3pm in the afternoon, there was a joyful re-union with Ivy and Margaret. The day's journey ended with the 80 mile drive to Kawimba, arriving at 10pm. There is no mention of falling into bed exhausted but rather a time of thanksgiving and fellowship with others there. Then 'a comfortable night before leaving for Nyankanda at 7.30am, and arriving there about noon.'

'So ends another eventful trip, one of great interest for me. I hope, one of profit for those I met. Again I experienced the feeling that "Underneath are the everlasting arms". (Deuteronomy chapter 33.verse 27), and that 'all is well and the heart is at peace'

NYANKANDA

It was no time before he plunged in to the work at Nyankanda again. He was glad to have Dr. Allan Bapty back again for 'there was much work for us to do'

The following day there was a trip to the Government Hospital.in Ruyigi, the town 15 miles away. Two patients needed X-rays and treatment for tuberculosis. While there he went to the Post Office to send off two cables. One was to his son Ian, to congratulate him on his engagement to Marion.

Back in Nyankanda work continued but Saturday afternoon there was lull in hospital activities. Bob and Allan walked the three and a half miles to a waterfall, which was to be the site of a hydro-electric scheme. Meanwhile Margaret walked twice that distance with Dorothy Lowe, to visit a village church in the bush.

After a quiet Sunday, with not even a talk given, it was back to work at top speed in the hospital again, refreshed by the break and rest. Bob continued to have the assurance that Allan was the right person for Nyankanda. He was also very impressed with the simple faith of the African Christians. The fact that they have had the Scriptures in their own language for such a short period, made their Bible knowledge even more impressive. Still they only had the New Testament and not the Old.

Important decisions had to be made by the Board which met, and where Bob's report had been read. There was much prayer for the decisions taken, for all wanted them to be according to God's Will, and for there to be unity of purpose.

The last evening there a Prayer Fellowship expressed this unity of purpose beautifully. So the sad day came for packing and departure. But before leaving a short time was spent with the patients. Most of them assembled to say farewell. Of the three months it was said 'it was a rich experience. I did not achieve all I had hoped. There is every possibility of its development to be worthy of the Lord and fulfil His purposes. For this I am profoundly thankful. I have learnt much. We leave with a much better appreciation of the work of the Lord in this place.'

By 2pm they were on their way with the Station Wagon loaded to the gunnels. Indeed it was so loaded that even in low gear it had great difficulty in getting up some of the steep hills. Was it really that the engine required tuning?

The halt at Matana gave time for a catch up on letters, and to complete correspondence. However the altitude did not suit Ivy so plans to move on were accelerated. This hospital where Allan worked was important. The possible move of the nursing sister away was, therefore, regrettable, leaving Allan with even greater responsibility and strain,for his remaining time, prior to leave and moving to Nyankanda.

Clearly Bob enjoyed the driving and certainly shared it with the driver. The rough drive of an hour and a half to the barrier took them very near the edge of escarpment in many places, to avoid the pot-holes. 'At another point I could not avoid one of the many pot-holes and went into it with considerable force, but 'Winnie' got out of the rut with no more than a heavy bump which did not seem to loosen anything.' So after four hours drive they arrived to a welcome cup of tea in Usumbura.

CONGO AGAIN

The relentless pace continued - cashing travellers cheques, collecting airline tickets and off to the airport again by 9.15am. After an unexplained delay of half an hour, the flight left for Stanleyville. The Sabena Airlines flight was subjected to a lot of turbulence due to heavy rain. Stanley and Mali Browne were at the airport to meet Bob. They went to see various Government officials before driving off to Yakusu in the evening. This took about an hour on the good road, rather than the two hours in a motor boat on the river, on a previous visit.

Time spent at Yalisombo was intensely interesting for both men. Bob had definitely found an ally in the keen mind of Stanley towards research. Here, too, was an abundant source of material to aid their study and advance in knowledge of this fascinating and mystifying disease. Some villages contained as much as 25- 45% prevalence of leprosy. Here this able physician and surgeon had not only material for research but a wonderfully dedicated team of workers. The combination of all this with a time of 'hands on' must have been a real fillip to Bob. Such a stimulus spurred him on. However he says, 'African leprosy is a most complicated subject, the more I see the less I seem to know about it.' Sunday was hardly a day of rest, for he spoke at the service in the leprosy settlement in the morning and was again leading and speaking at an evening meeting for the expatriates. There was, no doubt a late night and early morning gladly spent in preparation.

Work resumed with a vengeance on Monday morning as they set off at 6.15am on a circuit of 180 miles to visit clinics (dispensaries). The journey was mostly through dense forest. At each clinic a Christian African Nurse was posted. On the way they stopped to meet an African Chief, whose father had been a cannibal. He had refused to allow any alcohol at his initiation ceremony. The ills of alcohol were all too apparent with licences freely granted and the production of much native beer. As a Christian this chief was showing his disapproval of the excesses and ills of alcohol.

At the first clinic stop Bob was introduced to "Poor Pussey"- for that was what he was called. His real name was Pu-pusse Leon. The whole family and house were looking absolutely immaculate. This included the 'small house' (toilet). This comment came, no doubt, after Bob had 'emptied his radiator' as he used to call this necessity when travelling.

130 patients were seen here. It was clear to Bob that Stanley was much loved by the people as well as having a high standing with the Governement. Here we see another similarity in the two men, for the same could be said about Bob in India, and in other places where he had dealings with both categories.

Time together gave opportunities to share the problems as well. Sadly when there is a well functioning, prospering programme, jealously creeps in. Discredit and discouragement are two of the devil's favourite tools.

The leprosarium at Yalisombo was being used by Warner Brothers to make a film entitled "The Nun's Story" So Bob was able to meet Peggy Ashcroft, the famous British actress and one of the Directors. Contact addresses were noted for future possible use - never losing an opportunity.

Three more villages were visited and one of them had an prevalence of over 25% leprosy. Bob was delighted to find injections of Sulphetrone were being used with good results. These produced less reaction that the D.D.S. tablets.

Some who had been given D.D.S. developed a slatish blue discoloration of the skin which was intriguing.

This chain of clinics had been built up by Stanley and Mali, who cycled in the days of no roads and no cars - fine in dry weather but not in the far more frequent days of rain and mud. No wonder they were loved by the local people.

This development of clinics and village churches held tremendous potential both for leprosy and the Church of God, with such simple faith and dedication.

The centre of the work is the village church, the nucleus the school, and healing ministry an integral part. 'Seldom have I seen elsewhere this combination of teaching, preaching and healing'

Bob recommended an urgent evaluation of the work and longed to see a "Purulia" developed here to support Stanley's scheme.

The next day's journey took them to two more clinics where over 200 patients were seen. These villages had as high as 35% incidence of leprosy in the total population. The dry season ended with rain all night and a heavy thunder storm. But Bob was so impressed with Stanley and Mali who never missed an opportunity to worship with the villagers. As he saw it, this was an amazing opportunity for leprosy work to build and strengthen the church in a unique way. Indeed in later years this has happened in many places around the world. But back to the muddy, muddy roads which were travelled thanks to the low, low gear. Even then, in places they had to get out of the car and push it through the mud. They met a Government Officer 'who had been pushing his vehicle for 2 miles and said it was quite impossible to get through.' He did not count on the trust in God which had already committed the day to His Guidance and Safe keeping. So, even if they were mudlarks, they made it to the river ferry. This large, ingenious affair was pushed and guided by a motor boat. An hour's delay was caused by the wire from the motor boat getting entangled with the propellor. Fortunately the propellor was not damaged or they might have been marooned mid-stream. The prayer again came to mind "Let no trifles ruffle our temper, or disappointment unnerve us. Give us rather, a sun-shiney face, a forthright hand, and the joy of a word fitly spoken to some timid, discouraged soul."

'We needed this advice, for when we crossed the river, the road was still worse and it was indeed hard going, but we made it.'

Bob noted that villages near the river and further from the forest had less leprosy and wondered why.

Bob, who never mastered an Indian language, continued to marvel at the bi-lingual capabilities of Stanley and Mali. The Pastor of 52 years, who was described as a Christian Gentleman by Stanley, still remembered the dreadful days of cannibalism. His comment was 'Church Leaders have great influence in the World Council of Churches and this is encouraging, but we forget the simplicity of the rural church at our peril. It is frequently in the villages that seeds of communism are sown.'

The return to Stanleyville on Saturday afternoon included two ferry crossings, without any problems, and an easier drier road fortunately. A depressingly huge amount of mail was waiting so time in bed that night was brief.

Leaving on Sunday, meant finishing off pending work and missing church, but not elevenses with the Nursing Sister, prior to departure! She confirmed Stanley was most acceptable to his colleagues and therefore she found it hard to understand how certain difficulties had arisen.

The drive back to Stanleyville and the flight from there to Usumbura get a cursory mention. When they arrived at 3pm he was amazed to see a huge crowd assembled, including Chiefs, for the King of Urundi had been on the flight! Ivy and Margaret were also in the crowd.

On Monday 3rd February preparations and shopping for the next trip were made and then there was a party at the American Methodists to celebrate Margaret's birthday. The following day they left for Bukova at 10am. and spent the night there. The next stop was Ruannguba. Here the night was spent with a Dr. and Mrs. Humphreys. The view from their house of a mountain range included several volcanoes. One was active which made the view even more spectacular. Bob spoke to the students of the Bible School before they left for Albert National Park. After all the hard work and travel it is encouraging to learn that there was this happy interlude as a family. After a comfortable night in the Rest House the guided tour at 5.30am revealed elephants at

116

close quarters, antelope and buffaloes, but sadly, no lions. By 10.30am, after breakfast, they were again on the road to Katwa.

Here, they spent a week-end and then most patients were seen, photographed and biopsed, the ones with problems being helped.

So on to Oicha for a week. Here again many patients were seen. It was also the scene of research. The week was profitable and the time of fellowship with the family and their colleagues much appreciated.

Brief visits to Nyankanda, Rethy and Kuluva are mentioned before usual customs formalities at the border. A trip to Arua, 7 miles away completed the formalities. They were welcomed by the Williams. But which Williams we are not sure, for there were two bothers – Dr. E.H. and Peter. Between them they ran a very efficient work. One of them was trying to get some bye-laws passed to help prevent the spread of leprosy in the West Nile District and to encourage regular attendance.

A trip 100 miles to the north of the province, was only 12 miles from the Sudan border. Here segregation villages worked well. The tribes were grouped in clans. This system had worked well in Nigeria where Dr. Kinnear Brown established it. The District Commissioner was needing encouragement, and this scheme with the aid of the bye laws could provide it.

One day was spent writing up notes and dispatching biopsies to the London office taken in Nyankanda, Oicha and Katwa, 'so Mr. Wheeler is not inundated when I return.'

It seems that the Cochranes were staying with Dr. E. H. Williams, for one evening after supper they all went over to Peter's house for a prayer meeting. This was somewhat disrupted by a drunken crowd on their private road. The police had been called but took a long time to arrive. Meanwhile the three men stood still, refusing to be provoked. In the end the Doctor spent the night at the Police station to avoid anger being vented on the thatched roof buildings. All the Christian hospital boys lined up silently, ready to help if violence occurred. Bob felt this was 'a glimpse into darkest Africa.' Several Christian teachers' houses had been set on fire about 7 miles away.

The driver witnessed the whole affair and must have noticed the difference between the behaviour of the hospital staff and the frenzied behaviour of the drunken villagers. The troublemakers had come from a more distant village and were definitely the worse for drinking alcohol.

MURCHISON FALLS

A day was spent here seeing elephants, buffaloes, crocodiles, lions, a rhinoceros and many deer. There was not a good view of the falls from the launch, so Bob and Margaret went by car to the head of the falls. It was a remarkable sight, for the whole volume of water from the Victoria Nile fell through a chasm just 18 feet wide. It was all intensely interesting and 'I never want to see animals in a Zoological Garden again.'

Another long day's drive took him to Kumi. Here he saw a great improvement since his last visit in 1952, both in the children's work at Kumi and the adult work at Ongino. Dr. Maurice Lea was responsible for this. They spent the day peering down the microscope. The Nursing Sister Mary Stone had developed into a good technician preparing the slides and showed considerable photographic skill. Both skills appealed to Bob, and were encouraged. A quiet Sunday included attending early morning Communion, speaking at the 9.30 am service and attending Evensong in the Cathedral. After this he went round the General Mission Hospital, which included maternity and dental work. Another encouragement to Bob's desire for excellent work of quality rather than quantity.

BULUBA was the next place where again most time was spent peering down the microscope. 6 years earlier the work was efficient, but now it was even better. The Sisters were devoted and keen. The Mother Superior's kindness and humour were an inspiration.

ENTEBBE

There was a luncheon arranged at the Uganda Club for leprosy workers. Due to his self admitted impatience Bob tried to get there himself at 11.30am. The doctor arrived at the hotel to collect him 5 minutes later! Due to the help of an African on a motorbike and a friendly Indian he made it, after getting lost. After the lunch, there was a meeting in Makere College. Talks were given by an Orthopaedic surgeon and a Specialist in Tuberculosis and Leprosy, creating considerable interest.

Makere College appears in Ivy's Prayer diary on day 22, with the names Agnes and Fletcher Lunn and Dudley Dalton in her caligraphy. The beautiful setting of Lake Victoria was appreciated when there was a short tour by car along its shores. A Buffet Supper given by Dr. Kinnear Brown gave an opportunity to meet some interesting people including a lecturer from the University of Cardiff.

The next day in a visit to the Director of Health Services with Dr. Kinnear Brown the political situation was mentioned. This was not helpful to developing a research programme.

The work of Dr. Brown was highly commended. It included detailed work, education and awareness. He deplored, however his use of the banned word – leper. The usual argument for its replacement by 'leprosy patient' was firmly given.

KAMPALA

There he visited Makerere College. After his own efforts in Vellore, he was very impressed with the many departments. Stimulation coming from links with workers in Oxford, Cambridge and the Medical Research Council in London. Bob gave a technical lecture to senior students and staff of the college. He enjoyed a visit to the Research Station but regretted its location.

Then on to Nairobi, where the Chevrolet Carryall was left for sale. So on to Mombasa, where Ivy and Margaret sailed on the Rhodesia Castle back to England on March 28th 1958.

Meanwhile Bob, discovering the car had not been sold, took it and drove the 714 miles in seven and half hours back to Nairobi. He spent the morning with Christian friends and spoke at their meeting. 6.30 pm the same day found him aboard a Britannia aircraft bound for London.

So one of the longest tours was completed, In Bob's own words 'What more can I say than we started with some trepidation, wondering if it was foolhardy, deciding to motor through Central Africa and back to Nairobi - 7,500 miles.

We ended the tour with hearts full of gratitude to the good Lord, who had given us fresh evidence, if that were needed, that for those who submit their ways to the Lord, there are no coincidences.'

CHAPTER 12

RETIREMENT LOOMS 1964.

Work with the American Leprosy Missions Inc. included visits to Carville in Louisiana, U.S.A. Here the U.S.A. Public Health Hospital was a hive of activity. It was also known as the Gillis W. Long Hansen's Disease Center, and the only institution for the treatment of leprosy (Hansen's disease) in North America.

Patients moved around on electric wheelchairs, and staff cycled along the lengthy corridors between buildings of this expansive area. Treatment and social activities filled the days for resident patients. Staff conducted their professional duties in the various departments, like any other hospital caring for patients.

The Star magazine was produced, printed and posted off to the four corners of the world, every two months – 118 countries according to the July/August 1978 issue (vol 37.No 6.) A staff of over a dozen people from the residents kept this printing operation going. It included an editorial board, graphic arts and so on. The purpose of the magazine was to promote an educated public opinion of Hansen's disease (leprosy) and furnish vocational rehabilitation for interested patients. In the fascinating book "Alone no longer", Stanley Stein says of himself, "I certainly wanted The Star to be a friend to the friendless. But I dared not hope then, that it could ever become the voice of the voiceless, a cry of despair from those without the camp, an appeal for justice."

DAMIEN DUTTON AWARD

When the Damien Dutton Award was established, Stanley Stein was the first recipient. In 1964 the 12th award was to Bob in Carville, in the presence of Stanley Stein and many others, staff, patients, officials, and a previous recipient Sister Hilary

Ross.

In his reply following the presentation Bob called the patients "his beloved friends". He thanked them for their co-operation, patient endurance and bravery which greatly encouraged those who worked in the leprosy campaign. Of Stanley he said, "he has done more than any other person to dispel the unwarranted fear of leprosy".

See Plate 17 photo of Robert with Stanley Stein, first recipient of the Damien Dutton award.

Of himself he said, "In the last 20 years I have endeavoured to enlist the support of workers in the fundamental sciences in the study of leprosy. To some extent I have succeeded. We have a long way to go." He concluded his remarks by saying, "When we are as successful in enlisting the support of the whole medical profession as Stanley Stein has been of the public, then the day will rapidly dawn when suspicion and dread will be replaced by understanding and hope".

See Plate 16 photo of Robert with Damien Dutton Award in Carville.

This ceremony was held on 11th November 1964, a day observed as Veterans Day in America and Remembrance Day in Britain.

A letter was read out during the proceedings from President Lyndon Johnson, which he had written on November 6th

"Dear Dr. Cochrane,
I am pleased to extend congratulations to you on receiving the Damien-Dutton Award. The unselfish service you have rendered in the struggle against Hansen's Disease is in the finest tradition of your profession. Your contributions in the field of

leprosy treatment and research transcend all language and ideological barriers and promise succour and hope to millions.

My best wishes for continued success in all your future efforts as you work toward the worldwide elimination of this disease.

Sincerely,

Signed Lyndon B.Johnson."

By 1964 his appointment as Technical Advisor to the American Leprosy Missions Inc. came to an end. The extensive tours and travel were reduced. There was still plenty of work for the Ministry of Health as its Advisor on Leprosy. Travel around the U.K. to leprosy patients as a consultant and regular visits to the Homes of St. Giles in Essex continued. The flourishing Leprosy Study Centre continued to receive specimens from around the world to keep the laboratory staff busy. It also enabled Bob to keep a pulse on individual patients around the world. This all aided his research and maintained his deep interest in people affected with the disease.

1965. LEPROSY STUDY CENTRE

More dramatic changes took place as he retired from the Ministry of Health as its Advisor on Leprosy. Another big event was the handing over the Leprosy Study Centre to Dr. Stanley Browne, C.M.G. O.B.E. The earlier association in Nigeria had been established on that first 'fraternal visit'. It had continued with Stanley's involvement in the trials of drugs over the years. As recorded in the Munk's Roll Lives of the Fellows of the College of Physicians of London 1988, "When I showed him some villages where over half the people had diagnosable leprosy lesions, he could not believe his eyes. It was then, he advised me to concentrate on leprosy and abandon my interest in general tropical medicine."

No tribute to Bob Cochrane would be complete without mention of the driving force in his life - his Christian faith. He was a convinced Christian. He lost no opportunity of commending and sharing his faith. Some people might have thought him dogmatic and aggressive, but more admired him for his forthrightness and pertinacity. He certainly was unyielding in his purpose and held obstinately to his opinions.

Once all these many responsibilities were shed he could retire. But for him it was a case of "re-tyred for further service".

An earlier letter from Bob to the Mission to Lepers (now known as The Leprosy Mission) shows that his heart has always been for work in the Mission.

Writing to say thank you for the honorarium sent to him after he completed the writing of the booklet "Leprosy, its Challenge and Hope", he then explained that he had a full time salary from the American Leprosy Missions, so that any money he received for lectures or writing he did not feel able to keep himself, but put into the Leprosy Research Fund.

He wrote "As you know my heart is really in the Mission. It has always been one of my regrets that circumstances have so turned out that I have been unable to help the Mission more. In fact, the breaking of that close connection which I had previously with The Mission to Lepers has been one of my great regrets during the last ten years. I have frequently taken the matter before the Lord. I looked to Him to so order things, that if it is His Will, I shall find myself, in the not too distant future, more closely in practical touch with the Mission to Lepers."
(TLMI Archives 23.1.1961 to Mr Fancutt Editorial Secretary)

In 1961 He wrote the First Edition of "Biblical Leprosy - a suggested interpretation" followed in 1963 by the second edition, for the Mission.

A DREAM ASSIGNMENT

The first dream to find a cure for leprosy had been fulfilled with the widespread use of D.D.S. and other newer drugs being added to the treatment regimes for leprosy. It seemed that at last there was a fence at the top of the cliff, rather than an ambulance service at the bottom.

The second dream, a specialised hospital and research centre had been fulfilled in the establishment of the Research and Training Centre in Karigiri, in his much loved South India.

Another great desire of Bob's was fulfilled in 1964. The second edition of his updated book "Leprosy in Theory and Practice" was published. This time a chapter on Neuritis was included. He wrote to Dr. Neil Fraser, now in the head office of the Mission, in London, sending a complimentary copy. He felt that some of the chapters had not achieved the high standard he would have wished, but with many contributors, it seemed inevitable. It was the most comprehensive book on leprosy ever published, and it was hoped it would be helpful for mission workers on the field. It might even attract new medical workers to the field of leprosy. He would appreciate any comments or criticisms.

So often those nostalgic feelings of wanting to stay in one place to work had been expressed as he travelled extensively. Now it seemed that at last this dream was to be fulfilled.

1965 SYMPOSIUM ON LEPROSY FEBRUARY – MARCH 1965 BOMBAY (now Mumbai)

This contribution is made by Dr. Shubha Pandya (nee Divekar) "Dr. Cochrane was here as a Consultant, in view of his unparalleled clinical experience. Also because of the book "Leprosy on Theory and Practice" by him and Dr. F. Davey, and this was our 'bible'. My memories are as much of Cochrane the man, as Cochrane the physician. I picked up wisdom from some of the hints he dropped in the course of his conversation and remarks. Fresh out of medical school and keenly interested in tropical disease, I joined as Assistant Research Officer at a project on nerve lesions in leprosy in Grant Medical College.

I observed him examining several patients. I remember he always enquired about the first patch of anaesthesia (loss of feeling). He explained that such an area preceeded – by up to 2 years – the visible lesions. This taught me the fundamental importance of sensory loss in leprosy.

I was awestruck by his apparent nonchalance. He freely touched them, running his fingers over their patches and nodules. He would point out various features, using the tip of his spectacle arm, then casually putting the tip in his mouth. He was teaching me that leprosy is not wildly contagious.

See Plate 21 photo of Robert in typical pose after examining patient.

Lastly one of my most treasured memories: The day before his departure from Bombay he said he wished to say good bye to Dr. Khanolkar, the retired Pathologist. After some difficulty we located the house. Due to dementia he did not recognise Cochrane, or respond. But Dr. Cochrane affectionately embraced him calling him 'his old friend'. It was a sad, moving sight."

1965. Following the visits to Madras, Calcutta and Purulia, the time in Bombay also included a visit to the Tata department of Plastic Surgery.

Research was included and also surgery. Paul Brand and others had a good input to this section of the Symposium. Bob was not, however, in favour of surgical intervention for pain relief of nerves. Nerves in leprosy needed the very earliest signs noted, along with investigating the first evidence of the disease. Home visits can give clues to early cases. His assessment of the present approach was "an ambulance service at the bottom of the cliff, rather than a fence at the top of the cliff". He felt however, that with closer co-operation and a co-ordinated plan, there could be a fence erected.

1965 THE INVITATION

By the Autumn of this year a letter was addressed to Bob at the Wimpole Street rooms from the General Secretary of the Mission to enquire if Bob would consider going to Vadathorasalur, in South India to work. Ivy would be able to go with him and at last they would be able to work together as they had done in Chingleput all those years ago. There would be no long journeys and separations for lengthy tours. He must have been bursting to get back to Brighton and share this news with Ivy. Would her health stand up to it? She had a weak heart due to playing tennis at a high altitude in India. Would she be willing to go? So many questions must have popped in to his mind. As we know he had never mastered the Tamil language, but Ivy was proficient in it. She could communicate so well with the local people. She had been active with the girl patients in the Guide Movement at Chingleput and in many other quiet ways. He thought again of being in Vadathorasalur, when he had been so impressed with the work done there by the nurse Emilie Lillelund.

We can be sure he praised God for this opportunity of further service and back to his beloved India, to stay at last. Here was what he had dreamed of - a place he could stay in and work together with Ivy. Some problems had arisen there and it was felt that Bob would be the one to sort them out.

When it *is* God's Way, the plans then quickly fall into place.

This is just what happened. The plan was put to God in prayer, for His answer. It came with his added blessing of assurance that this was the right way forward.
By October the Mission had formally accepted the offer of service, with pleasure. It

also commended Ivy's willingness to undertake this two year commitment, in view of her recent medical condition. (TLM Archives 18.10.65)

It was not without great cost for Ivy. She had recently had treatment for spondylitis of the upper spine. This caused her pain and some loss of movement in the hand, which had the same appearance as that of some leprosy patients. She had to constantly wear a collar and type each day for exercise. As a medical secretary, this was going to be an asset for Bob, as well as essential exercise. The portable typewriter was high on the list of 'things to take'

One huge decision was to sell the lovely bungalow in Brighton, and store all the furniture. This decision was not altogether approved of by the Mission, but we know that Bob was a man of great determination, and felt this was the right course of action.

The following months were filled with plans and preparations. But also Bob was busy handing over all his duties at the Leprosy Study Centre.

1966 INDIA - FULL CIRCLE

This eventful year brought many changes, but it is hard to find any year in his life which did not, for his whole life was packed full with a series of great adventures.
The house was sold and the furniture stored. Packing of the many boxes had been completed with the help of the travel agent, to be sent by sea. Hand-overs and farewells completed they were ready for this latest adventure back to their adopted country. Once more they were within the fold of the Mission he loved. How wonderfully God was still planning their lives.

They flew to Madras and then by road to Vadathorasalur. It was brief stay for this was the hot season and it was difficult for Ivy to tolerate the heat coming from

England. So after a quick re-sort of luggage and a look at the house, they made the journey up to the cool Nilgiri Hills. (Nilgiri means blue hills).

May is also the holiday month for the families. Boarding schools are situated in these hills and so parents travel up to spend the school holiday together. In the hottest month it is always a joy to feel that first cool air when travelling up the hill road, or in the hill train chugging up the steep hill at a slow and steady pace.

So a house was rented for the whole family for the month. Ian, their son, and his wife and two children, plus Bob and Ivy. It was situated in a Tea Garden, so surrounded by tea bushes and trees. There was a very busy day opening up the house before Bob and Ivy arrived. Cleaning, unpacking all the household items as only very basic items were provided. Beds needed airing and making up and the hiring of a helper to do the shopping and cooking. Drinking water and fresh milk needed boiling. Food was purchased daily for without refrigeration nothing keeps long. There is no such thing as travelling light. A baker may bring biscuits and bread to the door some days and often, chunks of meat may come in a basket on a coolie's head - no such thing as a particular 'cut'. Fruit and vegetables in season may also arrive, as a welcome addition to the limited diet. Even local honey may appear at the door. Other supplies need to come from the bazaar such as flour and sugar, semolina (for porridge as no oats are available). So the holiday began – a first with their grandparents, for Murray and Hazel. After the holiday Murray would start at school and the rest of the family would travel down to the heat of the plains. Days passed quickly with walks, picnics, puzzles, board games, tennis and other game events in the community, meeting others and enjoying the company and cool hills.

One day for grace before the meal it was suggested singing "All things bright and beautiful" rather than the others used more frequently. "All things cold and miserable" said Bob. A chilly wind was blowing that day and the house was rather draughty. The heat of the plains held no dread for him. He also had to endure bland food rather than his hot curry and rice. At least he could add green chillies to his portion.

PARTING OF THE WAYS

The monsoon was expected in June and with it some cooler weather, but also rather humid, with much rain, so the air conditioner would be a great boon.

The journey down from the hills would take them through Madras. Here many friends and associates would welcome them back again in traditional style. One such person were the owners of the photographic business in Mount Road were very grateful for Bob's advice to stay put in World War 2. Bob's great use of photos of patients made him one of their best customers.

VADATHORASALUR

This name became abbreviated to Vada in the family for obvious reasons.

Bob immediately plunged into his work as we would expect. Ivy began to set up home in the Doctor's bungalow. The sitting room was a tasteful green, her favourite colour. She would talk to Thangavellu in Tamil about the day's menu and provide a small posy of fresh flowers each day in the sitting room. She awaited the arrival of the sea luggage as eagerly as Bob awaited his Hillman car. They came on different ships and when the ship containing the car arrived Bob was off hot footed to Madras to receive it. There were plenty of documents to show various officials, registration and insurance. More work had to be done before he could drive it back to Vadathorasalur.

Ian, Marion and Hazel returned to Purulia, West Bengal, after leaving Murray in boarding school.

130

DREAM SHATTERED

A few days before the end of July while the morning class on the verhandah in Purulia was in progress a messenger arrived on a bicycle with a telegram.

It read "Come at once Mother seriously ill with stroke, in Tirokoilur. Dad"

There was an internal phone system linking the staff houses to the hospital. When asking to speak to Dr. Ian Cochrane the reply came back, "He is doing a round on the ward. I will ask him to phone when he has finished". Another attempt produced a similar reply, neither he nor the nurses were used to being disturbed on duty by a mere wife, doubtless with some trivial problem. The third attempt was to say, "This is URGENT I need to speak to him NOW."

Shortly afterwards the familiar sound of the metal gate shutting announced his arrival at the house on his bicycle. Fortunately the office for South Asia was also based in Purulia at that time. So a visit was made to Dr. Victor Das in his office. He immediately put down the work he was doing and picked up a train timetable. Various possible routes were explored to get us to Madras as soon as possible. Finally he said "Can you be ready to leave in half an hour?" A cross country way by road and another train to Madras would be the speediest option. Back to the house, as fast as we could pedal our bikes to pack our bags.

A bedding roll was hastily opened and spread on the bed to throw in things to take. Another with clothes, bedding for the train and toys. Boiled water put in a kolshi (earthenware pot for drinking water) on a wooden stand, Bible, books and a few other essentials for the long journey, plus, perhaps a long stay for Marion as a nurse. All was very hastily assembled. It was all an unknown quantity. The hospital jeep arrived and we were off - grateful to be released to go, yet wondering what we would find on arrival in the south. The half hour to make all the preparations to leave had gone in a flash. Now there was plenty of time to think – more than 36 hours. Finally the train pulled in to Madras Central Station about 7 am on the morning of August 1st. One of Bob's good friends, Marie Buck, was there to meet us. She gently told us that we were not going to Tirokoilur but to Vellore, for Ivy had been transferred there.

At 9 am Prof. Jagadisan would come to the station and take us in his vehicle on the 90 mile journey. He would accompany us, for news had just been received that she had died that very morning. After his Hindu worship he would join us on this sad journey. After going to the waiting room, a wash and some breakfast, a wait till 9 am. Poor Hazel, already missing her brother away at boarding school and now being told that Granny had gone to be with Jesus, so we would not see her in Vellore, was sad and tearful. As promised the car arrived and reached Vellore about midday. Leslie Weatherhead was there to support Bob. After a snack lunch, a quick wash and change (it was a hot,dusty drive), we were all off for the funeral, leaving Hazel to play with some other children in our absence.

In India, funerals are always on the same day as the death. We wondered what situation we would meet when sitting in the train, but were not expecting to attend a funeral. But we did praise God that Victor Das was able to speed us on our way to reach Vellore in time to support Bob at Ivy's funeral. There are many entries in Ivy's Private Diary of Prayer with a name and afterwards - - 's Glory Day"

It was indeed Ivy's Glory Day. She was now with the Lord she loved and served so faithfully. Bob had been sitting with her all night, and time stood still for on the 31st morning he wrote in his Private Diary of Prayer, "Mother called to be with her Lord at 7.30am (with 4.30am crossed out) 1/8/66.

The most suitable words I can put are those of the widow of Pastor Yona "Jesus is Mine". It is true. Jesus is mine, even though I have lost the friend (greatly beloved) whose life I shared, and with whom I used to talk everything over. Yet Jesus is mine and I add, she too is His, and in that beloved Lord, we shall be united for ever."

The scrawl is even more difficult to decipher than ever, as he wrote these words from the depths of his sorrowing heart.

It seemed as if the whole of Vellore town had stopped to pay respects to the wife of the past Director of the Hospital and Principal of the College. After a brief service in the chapel the procession went through the town to the Vellore cemetery. Coach loads of students, huge garlands of fresh flowers, cars of staff and other mourners, completely stopping all other traffic. A simple wooden coffin had one wreath of flowers from Bob on its top. So the earthly remains were in Vellore, but her spirit was enjoying the reward of faith.

After collecting Hazel and a cup of tea, the four Cochranes set off for Vadathorasalur by road, past Moses rock and other familiar landmarks. It was a sad return after just two short months back in India together. So soon the dream was shattered.

Yet already a strong faith was showing itself in what he wrote. The following Sunday he had been booked to speak at the Vellore Christian College Chapel service.

When asked if he would prefer to be relieved of this duty under the circumstances, he replied, "No, I will do it". The impact of that message was tremendous, for all knew that only a few days before he had lost his most wonderful wife, friend, prayer partner and companion. The anticipation of now spending time together in the work they loved, with the people they knew and loved had been thrilling. Yet, now that this huge test of faith had come, he was able to stand up give the reason for the hope that was in him. His personal dreams may have been shattered but he was still able to share his faith. The students and indeed, all who crowded in to that service were challenged to do their very best and use their lives in the service of the Lord Jesus.

Jesus, who had conquered death and promised life after death with Him, to all who followed Him. Ivy's beautiful calligraphy in the front of his copy of the Private Diary of Prayer now bore their full meaning

"Within the veil, be this beloved, your portion

Within the secret of your Lord to dwell;

Beholding Him, until you face his glory,

Your life, His Love, your lips His praise shall tell."

This unexpected trip to Vellore gave the opportunity for Ian to have a needed hernia operation. He was quickly discharged and spent his convalescence sitting in Out Patients department at Vadathorasalur seeing patients. His Father's new car acted as transport from house to O.P.D. A bubbly four year old helped to brighten what might otherwise have been a rather gloomy household. Poor Hazel was plagued with boils in the heat. Beside the bungalow there had been a tank for soaking bricks during the building. This now formed a small swimming pool which helped considerably, both for cooling down and fun.

The next weeks Bob lived in a daze of unbelief that Ivy was no longer physically with him. His routine continued and he saw patients in the hospital, but somehow he was like a deflated balloon, or a sucked orange. It became clear that he would need some help when Ian and family returned to West Bengal.

The arrival of all the boxes by sea meant going into Madras to clear them through the customs. The boxes were then transported to Vadathorasalur where they were stored in an empty house. The task of unpacking awaited the arrival of Marion, more than 2 months later, on her way to collect Murray from school. Each 3 months she would journey to the south and stop off for a week to visit, encourage and do more unpacking. All Ivy's clothes and personal things needed to be disposed of. In the days long before Charity Shops were established some ladies were very happy to have additions to their wardrobes of new clothes. Missionary salaries were often stretched to provide all the uniforms for school and clothes for children, leaving little for the mother's clothes.

FRITSCHIS

Here several more threads are woven into the fabric of the story.

The arrival of Dr. Ernest Fritschi and his wife Mano provided this much needed help to "Uncle Bob".

Ernest with his great gift of surgery started the reconstructive surgery programme. The Physiotherapy department became a place of great activity for patients. Those preparing for surgery did their exercises and muscles were re-educated on those who had undergone surgery on hands and feet. Organisation of training days for doctors were planned. These brought Bob back to life, for he was never happier than when teaching about leprosy.

See Plate 22 photo of Dr E.P. Fritschi consulting Robert in Vadathorasalur.

Mano, with her skills brought life back to the rehabilitation section. Looms producing cloth for sarees, were again heard clicking and those less able patients were found sitting cross legged doing cross stitch on hessian. Articles such as mats to sit on, bags and other items began to appear.

The whole place was beginning to throb with life and purpose. There were problems, but Ernest had a wonderful way with people and of course there was much prayer. In addition to his surgery skills Ernest was an ordained Minister of the Church of South India. He was able to contribute in taking services and Bible

Studies. Bob was no longer the dynamic leader but quite willing to act as Consultant and share matters of administration with Ernest, relying much on his wisdom.

Bob had offered to work for 2 years and he was determined to do this, but it was extremely hard for him. Letters of condolence came in a flood and then a constant stream, as the news reached different countries where he had worked. Their arrival produced a mixture of gratitude and comfort, and yet they had the effect of increasing his sense of loss. Replying helped to fill the lonely hours in his room at night. The microscope also helped to fill some of the lonely hours.

Depression was never far from the door in this isolated place. He confessed that more than once he had looked at the water tower and had been tempted to climb it and end it all. So he came to yet another cliff edge in his life.

The Psalm which King David had written for his son, Solomon, was also speaking to Bob as turmoil filled his heart. He also was able to say of the Lord God "You love me. You are holding my right hand. You will keep on guiding me all my life with your wisdom and counsel. Afterwards you will receive me in to the glories of heaven." (Psalm 73 verse 20,22 and 23.)

Another of the Psalms, which was adopted by the Cochrane family as their special Psalm was Psalm 91. The promise of protection by angels had been his experience many times - as a baby, as a young man, as a young doctor, as a skilled professional advisor travelling the world, and now in his old age. The final three verses gave him the assurance he so much needed, "Because he loved me, I will rescue him. I will make him great because he trusts in my name. When he calls on me, I will answer. I will be with him in trouble, and rescue and honour him. I will satisfy him with a full life and give him my salvation."(Psalm 91 verse 14,15 and 16)

Among the many visitors who poured into the compound at Vadathorasalur came

Beth Wilson the Occupational Therapist from Karigiri.

SECRETARIAL HELP

Another thread now joins in the fabric. Bob always needed secretarial help and this came in a wonderful way. Judy Gough arrived in Vadathorasalur to give this much needed help. Her memories of this time there are now recorded.

"I met Dr. Cochrane when he was the Medical Superintendent of the Leprosy Mission Hospital at Vadathorasalur.

Dr. Cochrane shared part of a house with Ernest and Mano Fritschi and their three children. In the garden vegetables were grown alongside flower beds full of gorgeous Zinnias. Adjacent to the house was what passed as a swimming pool and once or twice "Uncle Bob" as he was known, would swim there with the two younger children and rather too many toads.

Mano welcomed us into her family and we ate all our meals together, with Dr. Cochrane at the head of the table. I remember that he refused to peel oranges – one of us did it for him.

He told us that he was the founder of the Chilli Club – to join the club several chillies had to be eaten at one sitting.

Robert Cochrane was renowned as an outstanding Leprologist. He was deeply concerned about the way those with leprosy were viewed by the world at large. He couldn't abide the word "leper" – it was banned from the vocabulary. He wrote a stinging letter to M.G.M. after the release of "Ben Hur" because of that film's appalling depiction of the disease.

Long journeys could be quite revealing. Dr. Cochrane was invited to speak at a conference in Calicut. The 300 mile journey in his Triumph Herald took 12 hours. It was on this journey that I learned of his meeting with Gandhi on one of his days of silence. He had gone to Sevagram to ask Gandhiji for money to establish a home for women and children with leprosy. Gandhi listened but did not speak, however he did send a large cheque.

Our clinics involved travelling some distance to check village populations for signs of leprosy. I remember that Dr. Cochrane used a feather to gently touch a patch of lighter skin to detect if there was feeling or not. If not, it was almost always an indication of leprosy."

Judy Gough typed many letters for Bob but not the increasingly personal ones to the doctor in Tanzania (who was later to become Bob's second wife).

LETTERS FROM AFRICA

Letters arrived from the many places where he had led teaching conferences.
Some came from those who knew him at the Kano conference in Northern Nigeria.
One came from a doctor who had attended a training conference in Iambi, Tanganyika (now Tanzania.)

"In the dry season of 1961 the Canadian nurse and I drove across country to attend. The days of teaching began with a time of devotions. Dr. Cochrane sat, as if alone with His Lord, worshipping.

His teaching made sense of this bewildering subject. I had been caring for the patients with a poor understanding of this complicated disease in Kola Ndoto Leprosarium. Bewilderment gave way to the excitement of comprehending.

Some participants left on Saturday morning to return to their own stations, others left in the afternoon. We were fortunate to be able to stay over for Sunday.

SUNDAY MORNING SERVICE AT THE LEPROSARIUM

Here Dr. Cochrane spoke, with translation.

He told of a time when he was in Eastern Congo. His wife Ivy was with him. She had placed a book at the bedside which he ignored.

The next morning he had no assistant, no translator, and was crippled without one. When the helper arrived very late he scolded him. Bubbling with joy, the man explained that the previous evening he had gone to resolve a disagreement. As they had talked and prayed together the disagreement was resolved and turned to rejoicing together. They were unaware of the passage of time and then overslept.

Now the work of seeing the many patients assembled could start. A great many were seen, examined and treated.

The next day the Assistant was prompt and received an apology for the scolding. The startling response was "Those are the sins for which the Saviour died".

"It was as if an arrow had struck my heart", Dr. Cochrane told a well filled church. That evening he remembered a situation which needed resolving. He spent a long time writing a letter to this person so was very late to bed. As a result, like the assistant, he then slept very well, so well he over slept. The African brother jumped for joy, not with any sense of getting even but as they shared their rejoicing in the living, forgiving Saviour, as true brothers.

It was an unforgettable testimony from an unforgettable person."

(page 45 of Aurora Lea by M.J Oldman). M. J. Oldman was the Dr. MJ Shaw in

Tanzania, who became the 2nd Mrs Cochrane. Then after Bob died, married again to a 90 yr old, also a resident in the Retirement establishment in Tennessee!

As the end of the two year period in Vadathorasalur came to an end, plans were made to go to Tanzania.

FAREWELL CEREMONY AND ADDRESS
Farewell Ceremonies are always big occasions in India.

An address is prepared and printed out to present to the person leaving, as part of the proceedings. Often it is framed and presented as part of a farewell gift.

This ceremony took place on June 1st 1968. We are not told who read the Farewell Address, but it was read and presented on paper with a border of lotus flowers. "Farewell Address to Dr. Robert G Cochrane. M. D., F.R.C.P.

It is with profound gratitude that we the staff of the Leprosy Mission Hospital, Vadathorasalur look back on the two years during which it was our privilege to be associated with you.

Vadathorasalur has been, for many years, known as a place which has demonstrated the Christian concern for those suffering from leprosy. During these two years under your guidance, we have had the joy of seeing this hospital developing into a comprehensive treatment centre for leprosy patients. This development has been achieved without any sacrifice of the personal relationship between patients and staff which is the hallmark of Christian service.

Your association with Vadathorasalur is not recent. In 1925, a year after your arrival in this country, you visited here in your capacity as the Medical Secretary of the then Mission to Lepers. During the succeeding years your life has been characterised by a

140

deep concern for the scientific treatment of the disease of leprosy, and liberation of the patient from the bondage of the social stigma of this disease. Your untiring enthusiasm in research, your unflagging concern for the patients, your uncompromising fight against prejudice and your deep Christian faith have been, during all these years, an inspiration to all those who have shared your concern for these patients. The modern interest of the scientific world in leprosy, is to a large extent, the result of your efforts, in stimulating experts in different medical disciplines to explore this much neglected field.

We thank you for having come to this remote corner of your adopted country. We thank you for the opportunity you have afforded us of being associated with you, and we take this opportunity of wishing you God's richest blessings in the years to come and a future of happiness and continued service. May He who has been your guide in all the past years continue to enable you to perform the task that He has yet in store for you.

The Lord bless you and keep you,

The Lord make his face to shine upon you and be gracious unto you,

The Lord lift up His countenance upon you and give you peace."

When the time came for Dr. Cochrane to leave Vadathorasalur, the Farewell Cermony was attended by all the staff and patients. The District Collector and the State Leprosy Officer were there. Messages were read from Dr. Dharmendra, Professor Jagadisan, Dr. Chandy and Dr. V P Das. Dr. Ernest Fritschi gave the vote of thanks. At the end of the ceremony, "wish you luck as we wave you goodbye" was sung. Garlands of flowers were hung round his neck, patients lined the route as he left the hospital and villagers lined the road beyond, all of them waving.

He left India for Tanzania on 4th June 1968.

There is also a photo of Bob with spectacle arm in his mouth, characteristically. On it he had written "To Judy with much appreciation of her help and friendship. Vada 30.5.68."

It had been given to Judy with the writing on it in his familiar scrawl.

As he left the hospital, patients lined the route and villagers lined the road beyond, all of them waving. He left India on June 4th 1968 on a flight to Tanzania." His luggage just a suitcase plus the brief case and a few other precious items, such as the MacArthur microsope and his Bible. The trilby hat lay forgotten in the excitement of departure.

CHAPTER 13

U.S.A. VIA TANZANIA.

Excitement mounted as 12th June 1968 approached. After 20 years as a doctor in Kola Ndoto at the Africa Inland Mission Hospital, Dr. Martha Jean Shaw was to marry Dr. Cochrane. A wedding dress, flowers and bridesmaid dresses were all assembled as the exciting day approached. Flower petals were laid in the bridal path by the youngest bridesmaid. Greetings and congratulations came from family and friends far away. The local much loved community were 'family'.

The new Regional Leprosy Officer made visits to many of the clinics in the 100,000 square miles of the District. Good relationships were soon established with Government workers by Bob's jokes. His limited Swahili and their limited English were overcome by friendliness. Successful leprosy seminars were held. A problem of Moslems wanting food after the cooks left at night, being Ramadan, had to be solved.

Trips to Shinyanga for offical work included the need for a Driving licence. After careful examination of all the pages of the UK licence, the offical did grant it.
Many adaptions were needed from life in China and India, but for one similarity, using the right hand to greet, avoiding insult, as left hand is used for toilet purposes. Africans are good at group activity, rather than Westerners acting as individuals. Their word for Westerners is wazunga, meaning those who run about dizzily!

INTERNATIONAL LEPROSY CONGRESS IN LONDON. 1968
Dr. Stanley Browne was very involved in its organisation, but Bob was President.

See Plate 23 photo of Robert addressing the I.L.C. London 1968.

143

Back in Kola Ndoto afterwards another seminar was planned. But with news of her ailing mother in USA, it was decided to go and care for her and support her Father.

VISA APPLICATION

In London a visa application was made for Bob to enter USA with his wife. All the required information from China, India and Tanzania was slow to come. Finger prints were sent to all the countries where he had lived for more than 6 months. Months passed as they waited in the Leprosy Mission guest flat in London. Finally it was granted on compassionate grounds when Jeanie's mother died. They reached Norristown PA on April 15th 1972 after a long flight and a long taxi drive from Philadelphia airport.

OFFICIAL HONOUR

After 6 weeks they were back in the UK to go to Buckingham Palace where Bob received the Order of St. Michael and St. George from the Queen on 17th July 1970. They took Eileen Ball as second guest, honouring her long faithful service as his secretary, when in London.

ROBERT COCHRANE ANNEXE

On 11th August Bob celebrated his birthday by opening the annexe at the Slade Hospital. The Block had 6 single rooms, a library, laboratory, offices and a large meeting room.

Patients with leprosy and other chronic skin diseases would be admitted for intensive investigation and specialised treatment.

See Plate 24 Opening the Robert Cochrane annexe, Slade Hospital, Oxford 11.8.70

.

USA

Back in Norristown arrangements were made for relatives to care for Jeannie's father so they could return to Africa.

KOLA NDOTO

Jeannie was fully occupied in the hospital and Bob endeavoured to improve the leprosy work. After the more advanced work in South India, at 72, lacking the earlier energy and drive he found it a difficult transition.

News of the carer leaving Jeanie's Father came, adding to this difficult situation they decided it was time to leave.

This huge wrench after more than 20 years was hard. "Go with Jesus" they said, and she replied "Stay with Jesus" in Swahili.

THIRD RETIREMENT

The journey to USA was via Eritrea. This enabled them to see Bob's daughter Margaret, her husband Peter and 5 children.

At last Bob was able to rest, being cared for by his loving wife. Many visitors came, filling 10 pages in the Visitors book. All were welcomed and given gracious hospitality. The International Leprosy Congress in Mexico brought more visitors including a previous colleague from his beloved India, Dr. Ramanujam.

Sadly he was too frail to appreciate all this attention.

Increasing ill health and periods in hospital followed. After 13 years of Jeannie's faithful care, his weary body died. He went to be with the Lord he loved and faithfully served 8 days before his 86th birthday.

Many obituaries recorded his great achievements in the National Press of U.K., U.S.A. and in India. However he valued most that his name is in The Lamb's Book of Life (Revelation 21.27)

His influence on others, both workers and patients, proclaimed his strong Christian faith and dedication to leprosy work.

MY LIFE IS JUST A WEAVING.

My life is just a weaving
between my Lord and me,
I cannot choose the colours
He weaves so skilfully.

Sometimes He weaves in sorrow
And I in foolish pride
forget He sees the upper
and I the underside.

Not till the loom is silent
And the shuttles cease to fly
Will God unroll the canvas
And explain the reason why

The dark threads are so needful
In the weaver's skilful hands
As the threads of gold and silver
In the pattern He has planned.

B M Franklin 1882 – 1965

AFTER WORD

Dr. Bob Cochrane helped to lay the foundation for modern leprosy work and I believe he would be very pleased to see the situation of leprosy patients and the treatment today.

The advent of Multi-drug therapy in the early 1980s revolutionised the treatment and care of leprosy patients. To me, these were the most exciting days in the history of leprosy worldwide. At last we could give hope of a cure to the patients, and really work towards the eradication of the disease and a world without leprosy. That knowledge gave a fresh enthusiasm and encouragement to most of those working with leprosy patients. Certainly where I was working in Bhutan, we were all excited about it, and were freshly invigorated in our work.

Since then the total number of leprosy patients worldwide has been considerably reduced, although there are many new cases being found every year. Now the focus of care is not only on treatment of the disease but on the causes and consequences of leprosy and on an individual, a family and a whole community.

Stigma is still a big problem in many countries, but with the emphasis on early treatment and prevention of disabilities, and on education of the general public, this is slowly improving. There are an estimated 2-3 million people around the world disabled due to leprosy, and The Leprosy Mission continue to carry out many reconstructive surgical operations on these people in order to improve their lives. Children with leprosy and those whose parents have leprosy are helped through their formal education. Students from a leprosy background are given vocational training in one of the vocational training centres run by The Leprosy Mission in India.

The Mission also assists in community based rehabilitation projects, like building low cost housing or renovating houses of leprosy-affected people. Many receive microcredit loans to help lift them out of poverty, and self-help groups are also assisted by the staff of the Mission. Research into leprosy continues to be funded by the Mission, and the great work is continuing.

This is because of the wonderful dedicated workers like Dr. Bob Cochrane, Dr. Paul Brand and Dr. C. K. Job and so many more who have given their lives to the service of God for leprosy patients. We, who have sought to follow their great example have cause to be very thankful to them for the foundation they laid for us.

Mollie Clark, MBE.

ACKNOWLEDGEMENTS

My special thanks to

- The Leprosy Mission International for Archives, including articles, addresses and reports
- Eltham College Archives and Archivist.
- Wellcome Library Archives.
- Memories of colleagues through correspondence, conversations and writings.
- Recorded experiences of other leprosy workers.
- L.E.P.R.A. Archives
- Archives of Sisters of Sacred Passion, "The Moroscope" and the Sisters kind help.
- American Leprosy Mission.
- The Star magazine.
- For permission by Dr M. Brand to quote from "Ten Fingers For God"
- Joyce Missing and Kate Whenray for computer help.
- Chris Hill for the photograph used on the front cover.

My great appreciation for the many helpers by prayer and encouragement.

Especially to Usha Jesudasan for willingness to use all her skills, great enthusiasm and interest to take the research forward but unable to complete before her death.

To John Whiteley for painstaking help as Editor.

To the Publishers for their help.

Last but not least, the presence of the Lord and the encouragement from His Word in the Bible, so applicable to my current needs, after planting the seed thought to attempt this book.

A big thank you to you all and to God be the Glory.

BIBLIOGRAPHY

Aitchison Margaret. *The Doctor and the Dragon.* The Chaucer Press Bungay,
      Suffolk 1983.

Baillie John. *Diary of Private Prayer.* Oxford University Press. 1936.

Brother Lawrence *The Practice of the Presence of God* Benediction Classics 2015

Buckingham Jane. *Leprosy in Colonial South India.* Palgrave MacMillan. 2002

Clark Wilson Dorothy. *Christ Rides the Indian Road.* Public Relations Dept.
Christian Medical College & Hospital Vellore S.India 1958.

Clark Wilson Dorothy. *Ten fingers for God.* Paul Brand Publishing. 1989.

Davey Cyril. *Caring Comes First – The Leprosy Mission Story.* Marshall & Pickering
      1987.

French Francesca. *Thomas Cochrane.* Hodder and Stoughton. 1956.

Greave Peter. *The Second Miracle.* Chatto and Windus Ltd   1955.

Jeffery, P. *Ida S. Scudder of Vellore.* Fleming Revell USA 1939.
      (Indian edition Wesley publishing Mysore 1951)

Levyson, Sidney Maurice. 1974. *Alone No Longer.* Funk and Wagnalls, 1963

Miller, A. D. *A Ship, A Ship.* L. T. A. Robinson

Oldman, Martha Jean. *Aurora Lee* Self published 2006.

Pewsey Phoebe C. *Honey out of the rock.* Antony Rowe Ltd. Whitlow, 1986